W9-DJH-232

JACK HAYFORD

THE LEADING EDGE

Charisma
HOUSE
Books about Spirit-Led Living

THE LEADING EDGE by Jack Hayford
Published by Charisma House
A part of Strang Communications Company
600 Rinehart Road
Lake Mary, Florida 32746
www.charismahouse.com

This book or parts thereof may not be reproduced in any
form, stored in a retrieval system or transmitted in any form
by any means—electronic, mechanical, photocopy, recording or
otherwise—without prior written permission of the publisher,
except as provided by United States of America copyright law.

Unless otherwise noted, all Scripture quotations are from the
New King James Version of the Bible. Copyright © 1979, 1980,
1982 by Thomas Nelson, Inc., publishers. Used by permission.

Scripture quotations marked KJV are from the King James
Version of the Bible.

Scripture quotations marked NIV are from the Holy Bible, New
International Version. Copyright © 1973, 1978, 1984,
International Bible Society. Used by permission.

Cover design by Eric Powell
Interior design by Pat Theriault

Copyright © 2001 by Jack Hayford
All rights reserved

Library of Congress Catalog Card Number: 2001095160
International Standard Book Number: 0-88419-757-3

01 02 03 04 8 7 6 5 4 3 2
Printed in the United States of America

Section 3 — Cutting to the Core
Facing Leadership Issues and Demands

[introduction]

If You Get My Meaning

THIS is a small book about a big subject—a role so often sought, a goal too seldom reached, usually by reason of misdefinition. Leadership is on my mind, but I'm asking for a couple of minutes on the front side of the book to explain what I mean by "The Leader's Edge."

As society views leadership, the quest for it is as common as wanting to be in front of the line, maneuvering to get ahead of the traffic, studying to top the class or cheating to attempt the same. Since lavish rewards await winners, human pursuits to "lead" foster a culture that breeds fierce competition—from corporate gurus leveraging hostile takeovers to parents manipulating five-year-olds in the fight for a Little League T-ball championship. To *lead* is defined as *succeed*, and success is verified by *conquest*.

That spirit has gradually ensconced itself in our culture's values—even in the arena I most serve, the church. There, as in most quarters, society's quest for the *winning* "edge" has produced deep erosion, so to write about the *leading* edge could suggest I was answering to these transient values.

Not.

I am hoping to point higher, deeper, further. To "get my meaning," take a look into *Webster's* with me first. There, *edge* looks like this:

> *edge* (ej) *n.* 1 : the extreme border or margin of anything; verge; brink; rim. 2 : the line of junction of two faces of a solid object; the sharpened side of a blade. 3 : sharpness; keenness; acuteness. 4 : *(colloq)* advantage. *–v.t.* 1 : put an edge or border on. 2 : sharpen. 3 : (often with *out*) defeat by a slight margin. *–v.i.* move sidewise; advance gradually.

As you can see, the options are broad, because a dictionary isn't telling us what a word should or did mean, but what this word means *now*. Consequently, since today's quest for an "edge" may drive an athlete to performance-enhancing drugs, an actor to backstabbing treachery, a businessmen to compromise or an accountant to juggle the books, it helps explain why some ideas about *leading* in church life have evolved and others been displaced.

For example, in defining *leader*, such traits as "trustworthy, steadfast, integrous and humble" have gradually given place to "creative promoter, striking communicator, growth producer or media voice." It becomes "all about winning." ("Of course," we in the church quickly assure ourselves, "it's all for the glory of God"; then we nervously clear our throats, uncertain of how convincing we sound—or worse, that we might appear either "overly spiritual" or "unpragmatic" in even showing concern.)

Now, please don't mistake my observations as either cynical or judgmental. They aren't an accusation or an attack, but they are *a shepherd's call*—defined by the role I've served for a near-lifetime. That role is the context from which I offer my discoveries of "the leader's edge"—living in the middle of *today*, but leading from the perspective of the *timeless*.

Those observations are also a disclaimer, something of a label on the box to avoid a reader's later disappointment with the product. If the "edge" you are looking for involves a search for better marketing plans, how to expand media pursuits, seeking to master event-production, gaining platform skills or unearthing the latest church-growth technique, you'll be disappointed.

On the other hand, if we've met by any means or media

before, my guess is you already expected what I've observed and aren't surprised at all. But whether or not we've met in one venue or another, let me establish what I see as fact— one word defines the essence of "leading," and that value underlies all I offer here.

Character

With forty-five years of *leading*—in *church* life as a pastor and preacher; with *teens* and *college students* as a dean, then president, then chancellor; with *men* at events from small breakfast gatherings to the October 1997 assembly of 1.4 million men on The Mall in Washington, D. C.; in *worship* as a composer, instrumentalist, teacher—I've had reason to settle on a clear and firm conviction.

Leadership is about *character*, and growth in character is what constitutes *the leader's edge*.

By "character," in a leader, I'm referring to a man or woman committed to becoming a growing *person* who grows *people*, a person whose *inner* life draws from an eternal fountainhead, so their *outer* life begets the durable (more often than the colorful) and the dependable (more often than the clever). Thus, leadership is defined not by *gifting*, though leaders are usually blessed with much; not by *intellect*, though even unwise leaders are not stupid; not be *opportunity*, since true leaders aren't produced by "getting all the breaks"; and not by their *charisma* or *classiness.* The latter may enable "coming off the blocks" quickly, but a fast start makes little difference in a marathon run. And leadership in that category isn't determined by who *wins,* but who *finishes*—who ran by the rules, was still standing at the finish and is ready to run again on another day.

So I offer you *The Leading Edge.* It's a collection of twenty-four articles in which I hope to point to principles that will lead leaders to "finish the course and keep the faith." I've arranged them under three sections—plus a finale. Most of them are from articles earlier appearing in *Ministries Today* magazine—a periodical I've contributed to for over ten years as senior editorial advisor. While they were first written to men and women whose profession is serving the church, my experience and acquaintances over the decades have taught me—"leaders" are leaders, *wherever* they lead.

That's to say, whether you're...

- **A football coach**
- **In middle management at a software company**

- [■] **Running a division in your corporation**
- [■] **Practicing as a surgeon or lawyer**
- [■] **Administrating as a high school principal**
- [■] **Teaching fifth graders**
- [■] **Operating a household**
- [■] **Raising a family**
- [■] **Working with paraplegics or Down's syndrome children**
- [■] **Titled as a bank president**
- [■] **Counseling teen candidates for Ivy League scholarships**

…you're deep into *leadership,* and I think there's something in here with your name on it. It's offered as something akin to what I do most of my time.

Today, having entered my middle sixties, I am spending most of my time with leaders—speaking to at least twenty thousand pastors annually during most years, and spending weeks at a time with small groups of forty to fifty leaders, one week each month at The King's Seminary in Los Angeles, where I live. I've spent these weeklong *Consultations* (over forty hours of direct engagement) with about a thousand different men and women in leadership. Being with them has helped shape the themes and selections of the articles that follow, for I've been as refreshed in my own leading in being with them as they suggest they have in being with me. It's an honor to meet, serve and grow with these shepherds of Christ's flock—people who lead with their lives, not just their skills. This book is dedicated to them, the participants in our School of Pastoral Nurture.

So come walk with me to "the edge," to a place defined by *more* than sharpness (though I hope that's increased) and by *more* than "ahead of the pack" (though I have no criticism for those who realize measurable success). Let me crowd you further toward what I see as "the leader's edge." It has to do with *heart* more than head, with *serving* more than succeeding and with *loving God* as the starting point for *leading people.*

Come; let's edge our way forward—together.

—JACK W. HAYFORD
OFFICE OF THE CHANCELLOR
THE KING'S COLLEGE AND SEMINARY
VAN NUYS, CALIFORNIA

Section 1
On the Point

Being and Becoming a Leader

"The Point" always involves a pivotal place and role in strategy. It may be the point man in the military, signalling directions that will determine the safety or effectiveness of a squad on patrol; the point guard in basketball, surveying the opposition and determining which way to direct the team and move the ball; or the person put "on the point" in a corporate project, whose experience, perspective and management decisions will determine accomplishment or failure.

After those parallels, it's clear people "on the point" are looked to—because you can trust them with your life, believe they have the team at heart and comfortably partner with their leadership because of their experienced track record.

These opening eight articles probe issues of the leader's growth at character stretching points, seeking to summarize the priorities essential to maximizing each of our *becoming*.

The Leader's Edge

There is no better place to begin focusing goals or sharpening priorities than to review the leadership style of Dr. Billy Graham. Unquestionably Protestantism's most notable personality and global influence in the twentieth century, he stands as a towering symbol of fidelity to the truth, integrity in character and constancy in his passion to pursue his mission. With it, let us set a pace—learning together as leaders. (Editor's note: This article received the *Florida Magazine* Publishers' Association award for excellence in 1997. It also occasioned the author's receiving a warm personal note of thanks from Billy Graham himself, after one of his staff pointed it out to him in *Ministries Today*, where Jack Hayford writes a regular column.)

For More...

As the twenty-first century has begun, many younger leaders are not as familiar with the remarkable, history-making impact that has been made by Billy Graham's worldwide ministry over the past half century. Two resources worthy of use for discovering foundational and inspiring information are *Billy Graham—God's Ambassador* and *Just As I Am*.[1]

[chapter 1] Let's Learn From Billy Graham

RECENTLY, a curious personal encounter reminded me what a remarkable gift the ministry of Billy Graham has been to the church around the world. This beloved and faithful evangelist has been both an anchor of reliability and a model of trustworthiness for nearly a half century of wide-spread ministry. As I came away from the conversation in which he had been mentioned, I began to muse over the question why. "Why is Billy held in such consistently high esteem by virtually everyone in both the church and the secular community?"

It's more than an academic question. In fact, I would plead with every Christian leader to weigh the values that are involved in the answer. It would be wonderful if every leader of any repute answered well to the criteria that have framed Graham's code of personal values and ethics in ministry.

In light of the phenomenal trust and respect given Graham by the general public, even through the season of cynicism we've navigated these past ten years, I thought it worth closer examination. How did this leader establish patterns of conduct and ministry, both public and private, that have produced a track record of fidelity in every arena of life and service? I was helped when a friend pointed me to a pair of analyses distilled in biographical works written about the evangelist. Although the two books were published twenty-six years apart (John Pollock, 1966; William Martin, 1992), they report the same abiding values pursued by Graham and his team.[2]

A rather unfruitful crusade in Modesto, California, in November 1948 turned out to be the catalyst that prompted the Graham team to set specific policies to help guard the ministry's integrity. The absence of community response to the crusade caused the team to seek God for reasons why. They asked themselves a probing question: "Why do people tend not to trust Christian ministries, especially evangelists?"

The result of their open-hearted self-examination brought six major areas of concern into focus: money, sexual morality, sensationalism, hyperemotionalism, digressions into temporary emphases or issues, and insensitivity toward the entire body of Christ—particularly to its local pastors and churches. Without taking time to sermonize or theorize on any of these points, let me simply amplify each by noting what is seen in Graham's ministry.

Money

Since the Billy Graham Evangelistic Association was formed in 1950, Graham has never accepted a love offering or an honorarium for work in his crusades. He would later accept pay for his newspaper column and royalties from some of his books, but his salary for his evangelistic ministry was set. He began with a salary of $15,000 per year, a wage comparable to prominent urban pastors in this country. That same standard has continued to guide any upward adjustment.

Sexual Morality

Candidly acknowledging their vulnerabilities to their own humanness and to the possibility of false appearances of wrongdoing, Graham and the team set strict, basic rules to protect themselves. These rules include: 1) Keep in close proximity to one another on the road—recognizing the mutual strength of both partnership and accountability; and 2) never, for any reason, be alone with a woman, however pure the intent (as in counseling) or innocent the setting (as in a ride to an auditorium or airport). Together the team would regularly pray, "Lord, guard us; keep us true, and help us be sensitive in this area—even to keep from the appearance of evil."

Sensationalism

Any study of the preaching, writing and evangelistic style of Billy Graham reveals a remarkable absence of the superficial, of hype or of pandering to the crowd or playing to the grandstands. Even in the early years, when his own youthfulness and his beginnings as a youth evangelist showed up in a more dramatic delivery, his communication consistently avoided exaggeration or "slick" remarks. There's never been anything cutesy or clever about his style. There are no grandiose claims or stunts employed to attract attention. Simply put, Paul's words in 2 Corinthians 4:5 seem to say it: "For we do not preach ourselves, but Christ Jesus the Lord, and ourselves your bondservants for Jesus' sake."

Hyperemotionalism

It is interesting to observe Billy Graham's balance in this respect. As both an evangelical and a Pentecostal, I have been encouraged by his steadfast maintenance of a middle road between the extremes of intellectualized sophistry and emotionalistic folderol. He is not afraid to confront people with the eternal issues of heaven's promise and hell's judgment, yet I've never heard him become either syrupy on the one hand or mean on the other. The plaintive strains of "Just As I Am" are a hallmark of his altar calls, but this unabashed use of so heart-touching an approach (which cynics would challenge as emotionalistic) is employed without apology. His recognition that the Holy Spirit does move upon human emotions is balanced by his commitment to let the Spirit draw people to Christ. Graham merely bows in prayer while seekers come forward—moved by God, not a manipulative appeal.

Avoiding Digressions

Billy Graham has written on prophecy, yet he has never been caught in the trap of sign-seeking, date-setting or charting the future and putting it up for sale. He has been at the center of our nation's moral and civic consciousness, having counseled presidents and called the country to obey God's laws. Yet he's never been snagged by a single political party, and he hasn't allowed himself to digress into any special focus on one political, moral or doctrinal issue. "The

Bible says..." has been his badge of authority and the bedrock of his ministry. He has always maintained his identity as a "Baptist evangelist," but there is not a sector of the church that hasn't been touched by his breadth of ministry. And here's the reason: He hasn't allowed himself to be crowded into narrow corners of "emphasis" that would preclude him from being a blessing to all—which brings us to the concluding point.

Commitment to the Whole Church

In the 1940s, when the evangelical movement was in danger of becoming ultra-fundamentalistic, it was considered congratulatory to blast modernists. Yet Billy Graham set a style that rescued the possibility of gaining some semblance of unity in the American church. He insisted that all churches and church leaders would be welcome—indeed, solicited and encouraged—to be involved in his crusades. From Congregationalists to Methodists, from Presbyterians to Conservative Baptists, and from Adventists to Catholics— all were received as partners for the sake of evangelism.

This largesse toward the whole body of Christ is also seen in Graham's commitment to the local church and in his love for pastors and church leaders. Cliff Barrows sums up his partner's attitude toward local church leaders: "He genuinely loves them and has sought to learn all he can from them; instead of criticizing their ministry, he tries to be sympathetic with the problems they face."

I was in my early teen years when Billy Graham's name became nationally renowned. I've met him, conversed with him in the circle of small groups of pastors and have been privileged to be invited to minister in the schools of evangelism he sponsors.

Although I've never been a close friend or confidant, I, like a multitude of other pastors and church leaders, have been profoundly influenced by his model of manliness, morality and clarity in message.

Psalm 37:37 says, "Mark the blameless man, and observe the upright; for the future of that man is peace." Being instructed by that exhortation from God's Word, it's helpful to have so ready a point of reference for follow-through. Thank You, Lord, for a man named Billy.

Jack Hayford, "Let's Learn From Billy Graham," *Ministries Today* (March/April 1995): 24–25.

The Leader's Edge

The leader on the cutting edge must discern between the enduring and the transient, between the essential and the expendable. Sound thinking that keeps in touch with the times must be characterized by a willingness to be stretched without allowing ultimate values to be snapped. A new millennium calls for leaders who will evaluate without devaluating, to define and refine their view without diluting or retreating from the demands of truth. In this article, I invite you to walk with me, as a Christian leader, and test the transient by the values of the timeless.

For More...

Those who deem the Bible to be the final arbiter on issues of truth, morality and faith must keep their hearts humble before its authority, but also keep their spirits sensitive to discern between ideas in transit and truth-unchanging. For over four decades, such writers as C. S. Lewis, Francis Schaeffer and Chuck Colson have been among those critical-yet-committed-to-truth thinkers who have helped me frame thought processes that inquire, critique and reveal flexibility, without becoming narrow-minded, cynical or slack. So much they have written—including biographical and fictional material—is abidingly applicable. I recommend such to keep a discerning "leader's edge" on the issues that finally count most.

[chapter 2] To Possess a New Millennium

FROM China's Great Wall to Egypt's pyramids, from Machu Picchu in Peru to the Times Square in New York, they greeted the new millennium. From balloon-busting parties to sushi bar singles' bashes, from stadiums to seances, the future was cheered—even if no one knew where it was going. And as the stardust of the millennial midnight madness settled, it remained for clear-eyed leaders to answer one crucial question:

> **Therefore, since all these things will be dissolved, what manner of persons ought you to be?**
>
> **—2 PETER 3:11**

I think our best answer can only be found if weighed in the light of two other considerations:

1. **How we think about the billions of humans who search for meaning amid life's transiency**
2. **How we shape our own personal world of thought and behavior to relate effectively to theirs**

The relatively recent turn of the millennial calendar

called more pensive minds to look seriously at the prospects for *world-impacting* and *world-changing* in the new century. This leadership call is obvious. To understand our role as one of Christ's chosen is to be here as His, and thus to be here for them. As His servants, I see our twenty-first century challenge not so much as a call to greater activity, but as a call to deeper transformation. According to God's Word, "changed into His image" people become the "shatter the darkness" people. (See 2 Corinthians 3:18; 4:6.) So "deeper transformation" isn't an escape into philosophy, but an entrance into a new availability—to Christ and to this new era's world of priceless people He is seeking to save.

Shake Out; Shape Up

To my view, the "glory to glory" work of the Holy Spirit in the church today is seeking to shake out the past and shape up the future. I sense Him seeking to shape my mind-set, and thereby my lifestyle, on at least four fronts:

1. **Expand my penetration through purification.**
2. **Examine my presuppositions with humility.**
3. **Establish my home as a center of warmth and light.**
4. **Embrace the price of spiritual passion without reserve.**

ON THE POINT—BEING AND BECOMING A LEADER

As a fellow leader, let me invite you to weigh these issues with me.

Penetration through purification

Expanding the future effectiveness of evangelization will require a detoxification of most of us in the church. Holiness of life is a prerequisite to spiritual penetration. The darkness doesn't yield to shadows but to Son-light. We don't need to meet high levels of religious performance, but we may well need to submit to a reduction of high levels of spiritually toxic residue in our souls.

I can't change the world if the world has changed me. If I've been blunted by bumping around in the shady areas that abound in today's sin-dominated environment, I have no penetrating power against the darkness. Sin has never been more sinister in its subtlety, neither have demonic devices ever been more effectively ensnaring. From the rawness of the shabbiest and cheapest to the sophistication of society's most elegant invitations to indulgence, the mind and the flesh are daily summoned toward seduction.

If no other finger beckoned, the lone potential of "electronic sin" is adversary enough. There is more than porn on the Internet. Sin is available from waste to wantonness, from seemingly harmless but life-dissipating wanderings in cyberspace, to the insidious wickedness of chat-room forays and e-mail flirtations that lead people to compromise their marital commitments and ruin families.

Or has the Holy Spirit dealt with you about your entertainment habits, as He has me? Having been freed from religious legalism regarding movies, have you ever found yourself vulnerable to an erosion of Holy Spirit substance in your soul? Has an undiscerning freedom from one extreme opened you to bondage by exposure to another?

Be it stage, screen, TV or video, there's a place where each of us who seek to penetrate the world with light must beware of incipient darkness seeking to dim our light and dull our focus. I have to keep free from the soul-wasting effect of the godless giddiness I encounter while seeking to enjoy simple comedy. I must avoid the abounding sexual innuendo present in virtually all drama today. I need to keep myself from the profuse profanity, blatant blasphemy and sensitivity-numbing violence that are included in the price tag of a brief excursion into an adventure flick.

Simply put, to function with spiritual authority requires that I live in purity. For example, my intercessory prayer cannot prevail above the levels of my own tolerance of sin in my life. To break strongholds in the darkness requires their being uprooted from my own life. Holiness does more than keep my vessel clean—it overcomes the sludge that slows the flow of divine grace through me, and it breaks the snares of hell that can neutralize my readiness for spiritual warfare or witness.

Examining presuppositions

I have found it is often risky to ask believers to "think," not because we are less capable than others, but because some of our convictions have too often remained only half examined. Without providing detailed discussion here, let me simply lay on the table some issues I believe Bible-centered believers will be forced to reexamine as we broach the challenges of the new millennium.

For example: Is it possible there is a meeting place between the truth of "man as special creation" and the ideas of "prehistory evolution," while still believing every word in the Bible is true? (I think so.) Is it possible that militant feminists are at least right in blaming "the church" for ensconcing male chauvinism? Could it be that radical racists are on the mark in their charges that religious traditions have dulled actions needed against discrimination? Is it possible that the economically deprived too seldom find leadership for their cause among affluent Christian businesspeople, and that the socially disenfranchised are too readily dismissed as "responsible for their own problems" by conservative evangelicals like me? (Tough questions to answer.)

Is it possible that not all homosexuals are perverted "haters of God," that greater discernment in my love and patience with all human brokenness is something God's Spirit might teach me instead of allowing me to quarantine sectors of sin from my available graciousness? (Probably? Or certainly!)

Is it possible for me to show a humanly warm respect for Muslims, Hindus, Jews or Buddhists? Is it further possible for me to honor each one's personal sincerity and intensity of commitment while still retaining my convictions about the finality of Jesus Christ as the world's only Savior and the ultimacy of each person's accountability before God's throne of final judgment? (Briefly... can "light" win people more effectively than "heat"?)

To be invited to engage such thinking can enrage the supposed "scriptural purist." But none of these lines of thought lead beyond the Bible's borders, though they may stretch mine. To think more thoroughly may enable us to reach more graciously. God's Spirit won't call us from the Word, but He does often require us to examine again some things we have been too cocksure about. I believe we will need to submit to such probing as this if we are to respond to His calling us into the new millennium.

Establishing "lighthouses"

The suction of most systems surrounding us points to the demise of regard, if not respect, for God's intended order and blessing for "the family." I need not itemize those politico-philosophical advocates, programs or lobbies "reinventing the family." But the fact remains that the church may not be successful in its effort to construct "breakwaters" against these tides.

To step into the new millennium as "children of God...in the midst of a crooked and perverse generation," we are wisest to cease cursing the darkness and focus on shining "as lights in the world, holding fast the word of life" (Phil. 2:15-16). We may lose the political war over "family values," but we can still win the spiritual battle if we commit to establish our homes as centers of warmth and light. As a believer, and as a leader, I need to practice and teach a new, young generation of parents how to handle "family building," especially since so many things work against them. Some of the challenges include:

- **The demands of double-income family-funding erode time for necessary interpersonal, life-shaping contact with kids and for nourishing intimacy between husbands and wives.**
- **The convenience of fast-food outlets plays out against the likelihood of life-to-life "knitting" taking place at a regularly sustained family dinner table.**
- **The schedule-separating structures of social, educational and recreational demands tend to dictate an allegiance "beyond all," displacing habits of wisely prioritizing home and church activities.**
- **The urbanization of society and the business of life distance us from contact, then concern, and finally from compassion for our neighbors—thereby removing our sensitivity to one of God's two summary commandments.**

This is only a "starter list" of issues, but they remind us of God's call to "not be conformed to this world, but be transformed" (Rom. 12:2). Why? Because inevitably, the world "hits the wall" by reason of its ruinous pursuit of human wisdom and ways. If we build homes that are aglow with God's love for one another, His light of truth shining from our windows and His grace pouring out toward our neighbors, the world will beat a path to our doors.

As individual parents and as vital congregations, the challenge of the new millennium calls us to build homes and families—havens of relationship-wholeness to which multitudes coming in from the cold of mangled relationships will be attracted, and thus find their way into God's forever family.

Embracing the price of passion

Finally, the new millennium calls me to cultivate a "kingdom mind-set" regarding borders of evangelism, my handling of my money and my availability to unapologetic, Holy Spirit-filled life and worship. The challenge to Christians in the twenty-first century is either to learn or to not forget the lessons of the twentieth—that is, the fire of Pentecost is the flame that lights the brightest, shines the farthest and burns back the darkness most effectively.

It is not a sectarian observation I make. The facts of church history as well as the trends throughout the whole church today—whether Pentecostal or Charismatic or not—cannot be denied. To "seize the day" we need to be seized by the Spirit! I'm not calling for "seizures," but for surrender; for letting go enough of my clutching fears or my cloying pride to give in to the grip of God's power in and purpose for my life, my thoughts, my service and my giving.

This will probably mean such things as:

[■] Letting Him broaden the boundaries of my vision for the world—perhaps to see for the first time that it includes the dying cities of my own nation, where the urban poor need churches and need an "in-reach" from outside congregations. Thriving suburban churches are not a sin, but ones with no mind-set for urban evangelism may be.

[■] Letting Him "break up the fallow ground" to renew my prayer life "in the Spirit," enabling intercession for global hot spots where spiritual weaponry alone will break strongholds and allow the gospel to advance (Eph. 6:10-20).

[■] Rededicating my finances to Jesus, realizing that He's seeking more than my tithe. He's seeking to lay claim on a generation's bank accounts, not to siphon off our retirement funds, but to break the self-preserving fear that always whispers, "You'll not have enough," and thus stifles liberality in giving.

[■] Rekindling the flame of passion in my worship, that I may come alive to His presence without pretense and to His power without reserve.

Yes, the world marked a new millennium in some creative and expensive ways. Now the challenge to insightful

Christian leadership is to invite the creative limitlessness of the Holy Spirit's power to overflow us—and to be willing to spend everything we are and have for Jesus' sake—and for the world He loves.

Jack Hayford, "Changes for the New Millennium," *Ministries Today* (January/February 2000): 20.

The Leader's Edge

History justifies the fact that a leader with spiritual values *is not* an unwelcome commodity in the secular arena. Spiritual leaders with small souls or bigoted minds, inconsistent standards or loveless attitudes *are*. There is a difference between "the world" as a corrupting spirit and "the world" as the general body of humanity who needs leaders with worthy values, unselfish methods and enduring goals. It is worthwhile to periodically pause, reflectively assess and carefully reenunciate what I believe I am called to be and become as a leader. Such articles as this are but one device to press others to consider this—and to "hold fast to the eternal."

For More...

Through the years I have been stirred with inspiration, stimulated with courage and shaped with deeper conviction through reading across the spectrum of leaders—from Winston Churchill to A. W. Tozer, from Abraham Lincoln to John Wesley. Simply to read renowned quotations of these men is to find ignition; to steep one's mind in their best thoughts is to confirm long-lasting, practical wisdom.

[chapter 3]

What the World Expects From Leaders

SEVERAL years ago, journalist Diane Sawyer and ABC's investigative troops mounted an assault on purported violations of ethical and economic propriety by television ministers. *Should we be listening to what the world's media has to say?* Whatever you may feel about that report—and others like it—in my thinking, my spiritual leader-mind has to draw at least one conclusion: The world expects something of us it doesn't feel it's always getting.

Sure, I agree that the "prince of the power of the air" does attack kingdom enterprises, and I have no doubt the devil delights when a jaundiced journalist bashes a spiritual leader. I have no judgment to make—only a judicious decision for my own part: *listen.* Somewhere above the scorning commentary and mocking laughter emanating from the world there just might be a message for us—if we'll listen for the whispered lessons from the Holy Spirit.

I'm not about to commend a pagan culture for its acidic

attitudes toward God, Jesus, the Bible and the church. But I think it's escapist to attempt to write off all that's taken place regarding media ministries as simply "an attack."

On the one hand, I agree with the proposition that Jim Bakker's sentencing (even when reduced) appears horribly unjust when compared with the vastly shorter terms of punishment given Ivan Boesky and Charles Keating for their convictions of financial scandal. But on the other hand, beneath the surface of it all—however brutal or unforgiving its demeanor—I think I hear a society declaring its *disappointment* more than its disdain.

"We'd like to believe in your God," the world cries. "But when you claim faith and still disregard His standards, you not only reinforce our doubts, but you also justify our holding you to the moral requirements of the God you claim to serve."

I've been gestating on feelings about this for a long time, and I have deep and serious thoughts about what God may be saying to me through such things.

Pure Motives

First as a pastor (and quite besides the fact that I also host a television ministry with a budget to meet), I think I'm hearing the rumbles of an honest question being expressed about church fund-raising—one as likely to be asked by my own congregation as by the unconverted.

Fundamentally, it goes something like this: "If you are so sure your God provides, why would you ever compromise in a mood or by a method that suggests your appeal is to assure a ministry's survival? If you believe God is sovereign, could your lack of funds be an evidence of His disinterest in your project rather than a prompting to make a frantic plea for support?"

From a biblical perspective, such questions are just. We are wise to ask them of ourselves. We are promised God's sufficiency and abundance 1) as we are faithful to obey the truth ourselves and feed our flocks with integrity of heart; and 2) as we walk and lead with a manifest trust in God's power and providence. Yes, it is a real part of our task to teach God's Word on the principles of giving and financial stewardship. But my ministry style must manifest that my motive is always the blessing of the sheep—and not merely the meeting of the budget. The difference between *feeling* and *fleecing* the sheep is not difficult to detect. If anyone smells something less than the fragrance of a pure motive, it's not only understandable that they protest—but also it could be God's voice to us when they do.

Accountable Lives

Second, every round in the media contains a repeated, louder-than-ever trumpet blast from heaven: The unaccountable life will ultimately be called to accounting. Again, my observation is not upon the relative right or wrong of those directly probed by a TV network. I'm simply trying to hear God speak to me.

People will tolerate unworthy critics or practices in leadership if we allow them. People aren't stupid, but they are sheeplike. It's essential that even the most faithful shepherds make themselves accountable to fellow shepherds, even if their flocks or immediate peers don't require it. Whether we like it or not, we are vulnerable to our own capacities for self-deception. We need the discipline of welcoming others into our lives to help us measure our motives, and to partner with us in living out the 1 John 1:7 principle of transparent fellowship.

Humility

One last thing: Doesn't it bother you that the most visible

group taking their lumps via the media are we who preach a full-orbed message of miracle grace and power? Sure it does—and none of us are immune to the pain and problems that overflow everywhere when such broadcasts are aired. So how do we respond?

First, let's not react self-righteously or with a quick pharisaical side step to the other half of the road. Even when I am unsupportive of a man whose life or methods have brought him under accusation, I remain cautious about adding my voice to those who are against him. I may not endorse a ministry, but that doesn't require my denouncing it.

Second, whatever issue may be raised in the scrutiny of others, let us always listen for the Spirit's voice to us. Only through the humble posture of a listening heart can lasting qualities of leadership evolve in our characters.

Jack Hayford, "What the World Expects From Pastors," *Ministries Today* (March/April 1992): 22–23.

The Leader's Edge

Few concepts sound less inviting on their surface than the biblical idea of *submission*. Not only has the word been twisted or warped by misdefinition and oppressive application, even its right and wise meaning and adaptation confront a "leader-type" with a reality some blindly deny. We all need accountability; we all need the protection and wisdom of others to balance us.

This article was written in the aftermath of being called into the "burn ward" where an outstanding leader had, through willful folly, placed himself. His self-destruct tactics are avoidable—and to acknowledge the wisdom of submission is not to surrender one's gift of either creative, dynamic, entrepreneurial skill or holy insight. Rather, it is to find clearer focus, refined direction and enduring influence—for good.

For More...

Though deeply believing in the desirability and importance of "releasing" leaders to realize their maximum potential, I have also learned the biblical wisdom that "it is good for a man to bear the yoke in his youth" (Lam. 3:27). The joys of being granted great privilege have been preceded (and interlaced) with the will to live a life of submission, interdependency and accountability. From that context, I offer two audio studies: "The Leader Jesus Trusts" and "Relational Priorities."

[chapter 4] Danger: The UVI Is High Today!

WHEN the local TV weather guru says, "Today's UVI shows that between 10 A.M. and 5 P.M., severe burning can begin after only seven minutes," more and more citizens take notice. The benefits of regarding the "Ultraviolet Index" can mean more than mere comfort the day after a trip to the beach or the park; it can even save your life eventually—avoiding skin cancer's complications.

Such physical-realm warnings flashed through my mind recently after more than a week of wearying involvement with a situation caused by neglect of spiritual warning signals. The board and staff of a ministry, as well as a number of people influenced through it, had occupied much of the time of a team of elders from our church—you might call them "burn victims." This "UV" wasn't ultraviolet, but was the impact of the "ultra-vicious" hellishness that deception can produce. The willful sin of a deceived leader had exposed many of those closest to him to hellfire—and they were scorched.

By "hellfire," I'm not talking about the eschatological type—the "forever-in-Gehenna" ultimate judgment. But a whole band of good people were now exposed and suffering because of disregarded warning signals to the potential of demonic "laser" activity when principles of "proper covering" are not in place.

Most frustrating among all we encountered in dealing with both the leader and the followers was that it all should never have happened. The realities of human vulnerability to the "star syndrome" seemed at the root of the "burns." I mean, the license to unaccountability that often attends the undue elevation of a leader's status in the eyes of those he leads—and in his own view of himself. These burn victims wouldn't be suffering the pain, disappointment, anger or confusion so many are if two primary principles had been regarded:

- [■] **If the leader had been willing to receive the warnings given or to honestly accept the accountability to which he claimed to be submitted**
- [■] **If his board or immediate staff had insisted more pointedly that he show a more complete stand under the protective covering of his acknowledged authority**

Instead, a lot of people have burns with varied degrees of hopeful prognosis as to ready recovery—the leader is in rebellion, two marriages are a mess, a ministry is torn by turmoil and economic strain, and incredible amounts of time are being exhausted by our elders, like an overtaxed hospital staff following a local explosion.

In God's grace, full recovery is not beyond hope, but it is so regretful that two fundamentals were bypassed. Like negating the weatherman's warning, the leader and those he led refused *both* a) to heed the warnings—such as "admonish one another" (Rom. 15:14); and b) to stay "under cover"—such as "submitting to one another in the fear of God" (Eph. 5:21).

When these affects of the "star syndrome" take effect, burns are inevitable. The radiation fallout of Satan's enterprises is devastating whenever he succeeds in deluding a spiritual leader or his followers, and a fiery independence leads to a path of Garbo-like, "I vahnt to be alone!," or a Sinatra-esque, "I did it my way!" Such "stars" may reign for a season. But you can be sure of this: Soon, like an exploding sun, their whole system will collapse into itself, and a black hole will begin to suck those near them into the vortex of its darkness.

Dealing with the aftermath of this "shooting-but-now-shot-down-star," I'm wanting to shout very loudly: "Church! Listen to the Bible's UVI 'burn warnings' and heed them!"

- [■] Require yourself and your leaders to solidly adhere to the Word of God and to keep biblical wisdom applied in all lifestyles and relationships. (See 1 Timothy 1:18-20; 2 Timothy 2:14-18.)

- [■] Require yourself and your leaders to submit to the confrontational care and admonishing accountability available via God-given elders, brothers and sisters placed around us, *not* to exercise suspicion, but to provide support. James 3:13-18 points toward the care that confronts but isn't brazen or overbearing in an inquisitional spirit.

- [■] Refuse to insist on your own way. Choose to suspect your own perspective when warned. Accept the cautioning signs given by either the Holy Spirit or others. (See Proverbs 18:1; 27:6.)

- [■] Never—never, never—forget how vulnerable all our hearts are to deception (Jer. 17:9). Let none of us suppose ourselves so wise as to believe an independent spirit or a self-serving pursuit is survivable. (See 1 Corinthians 10:12.)

- [■] Keep clear on this fact: *Who we are and how we relate to our spouse and family are infinitely more important than the way our ministry seems to be advancing.* Apparency of spiritual achievement is, by itself, never a verification of the validity of a ministry. (See Matthew 6:22-23.)

Through the years, I've let myself be shaped by watching and learning from great and godly leaders. Uniformly, they will be found to be "easy to be intreated" (that is, approachable and correctable—examples of true humility and authority in a balanced mix). But I have also watched gifted leaders come to disaster—crashing and burning. In these I have found one thing in common: the "burning" of refusing to "keep covered" came first. (Especially watch out for leaders who, if a loving approach of attempted inquiry or correction is made, threaten you with the words: "Look out that you 'touch not God's anointed!'")

We live in a day when the adversary is working against the clock (Rev. 12:12), and his Vader-like "death star" is radiating with a more ferocious intensity than ever. At the same time, our Morning Star is rising more radiantly in our hearts (2 Pet. 1:19). He's calling us to walk in His light.

Let me leave you with 1 John 1:5-10—it's a heaven-sent UVI warning for an ultra-vicious season of potentially dangerous exposure. It's clear on how to stay out of devil-rays, and how to stay in the one *Light* that never burns destructively—it only warms, grows and brings abiding fruit.

Jack Hayford, "Avoid Burns From Undue Exposure," *Ministries Today* (July/August 1998): 12.

The Leader's Edge

The ancient figure of the wineskins, which, once used, lost their capacity to be stretched again, is an apt one. It is employed by the Master in warning His learners against the soul-shrinking thought-and-life patterns of the traditionalists in that day. (See Luke 5:33–39.) He reminds us that irrespective of how true, right, wise or good are the ways we have learned, they can breed a smallness of soul that is unavailable to newness and a brittleness of heart that has lost its capability to love in truth and purity. In this article, I exercise transparent candor—not seeking to sound "so wise" as honestly confessing my discovery of "how small" I found myself to be—seeming to have forgotten lessons earlier learned.

For More…

Originally published over a quarter century ago, Howard Snyder's *Radical Renewal: The Problem of Wineskins Today* still speaks to the heart of anyone committed to lifetime growth as a person.[3]

[chapter 5]

When New Wineskins Start to Age

I was so disappointed! I was ashamed, embarrassed and frustrated. A cluster of personal failures had converged together to bring me face to face with frightening signs that my "once-new wineskins" were aging and becoming brittle—"old," to be quite frank.

The "old" doesn't necessarily refer to years of life—rather, in Jesus' metaphor, it refers to a cramping, tightening narrowness of the soul that has lost freshness and vitality amid the traditions of the flesh. (See Matthew 9:16–17.)

I was dramatically forced to recognize the "aging wineskins" syndrome. The confrontation came through what I now think might have been a sovereignly arranged cluster of incidents designed to expose me. They came suddenly, like a storm surge that sweeps on shore during a hurricane, within the span of about ten days. Their collective force shook me, driving me in their wake to a crushing self-discovery.

What most embarrassed me was that each of the tests I faced—and failed—was an inner issue I thought had been settled for me long ago. Early in the renewal that converged on so many of us one and two decades ago, I had either "put off," "laid aside" or "overcome":

- [■] **"That you *put off*...the old man which grows corrupt according to deceitful lusts" (Eph. 4:22, emphasis added).**
- [■] **"*Lay aside* every weight, and the sin which so easily ensnares us" (Heb. 12:1, emphasis added).**
- [■] **"To him who *overcomes* I will give some of the hidden manna" (Rev. 2:17, emphasis added).**

But suddenly I was overcome instead of overcoming. I felt like a once-renewed wineskin that was showing serious signs of brittle aging. I didn't like what I saw. And I'm sure Jesus liked it even less.

Handling Criticism

The first incident occurred when I was paraded in ridicule along with several Charismatic friends in a published work assailing the most visible leaders in this broad movement. Most frustrating was the fact that the broadsides were volleyed by a man I also consider a friend, notwithstanding his anti-Charismatic posture. In the aftermath of the attack,

I found the edges of my soul turning sour. My former will to live humbly and acceptingly with *all* Christians, however different in convictions, was cracked in the atmosphere of criticism. Suddenly, in private conversations with associates, I was defensive, retaliatory and moving toward a kind of bitterness I thought my earlier renewal had preempted as ever again being possible. But not so.

In a meeting with about two hundred of our congregation's primary leaders, I was stunned to hear words of barbed commentary about my critic—*from my own lips!* I did a fair job of recanting, but still, something tainting had occurred. I knew it—but I didn't know there would be more.

Drawing Comparisons

Not long afterward, I came across some statistics that should have caused my heart to rejoice: Our church was listed among America's one hundred largest congregations. But as I noted which churches were "above" us on the list, I found myself challenging the reported figures.

"Those aren't apples-to-apples stats," I said to one of our executives. "They're based on different computations and shouldn't be compared to our numbers!" Again, the "ping" of being surprised at my own words should have stopped me in my tracks. But I was now en route to a classic case of being exposed by God—of being unmasked by my words.

There was more to come. A few days later, I was speaking at one of the nation's great churches. While touring the marvel of their new, expansive complex, I felt an overwhelming intimidation. It wasn't jealousy (I'd face that about an hour later). It was a piteous recurrence of a sad, sad character weakness I thought I'd overcome years ago.

You see, I used to feel pathetically "threatened" when I heard, read of or visited the scene of a great move of God. A gut-grinding sense of intimidation would take over—an "I'm-a-nobody-by-comparison-with-all-this" sensation.

Years ago, I experienced a deliverance from this sorry state of mind. The Word of God quickened my senses: "Rejoice with those who rejoice," and "[be] not like those who compare themselves with themselves." Since that time I was always genuinely happy to see God doing great and gracious things whenever I found them—free of competition and without drawing comparisons to my own work. That is, until that day in that church. Then, within fifteen minutes...

An Attack of Jealousy

The *coup de grace* that finally brought me to the stark realization that I was on shaky soil in my own soul struck like lightning—twice at the same spot.

While visiting the office of that church's audiocassette ministry, I asked how many tapes were sent out weekly. The number I was told was *enormous,* vastly beyond the number distributed through my own teaching ministry. I should have been happy for such health and blessing being spread to multitudes—and I wanted to be. Instead I reeled under a vicious, wounding assault on a point of pride I hadn't recognized until then. It didn't overcome me—I *did* fight back. But I detested myself that so vile a spirit of jealousy could even momentarily taunt my soul.

All of these things stink, I know. And I can't say that it's any delight to reveal them—except that I can do so with an honest heart freshly freed through confession of my sin to God.

I thought this recommended my confessing to you, too. Why? I feel a special sense of mission to stand accountably before fellow laborers in Jesus' vineyard. To use John's words, I am "your brother and companion in the tribulation"

(Rev. 1:9). As such, I don't always fare well at first in every skirmish with either self or Satan, but I have learned to over-come—at least in the end.

With this, however, I wonder if my being exposed to myself by God—unmasked before a mirror and finding flesh revealed that I thought had long before been buried once for all—may have implications for you. I don't mean to accuse, in a misery-loves-company way, but rather to inquire.

Of course, not one of us is ignorant of the subtle skill of the old nature in resurrecting itself. It doesn't trumpet its ris-ing, but simply steals silently from the tomb and weaves its way with stealth and cleverness into new forms of expres-sion in our lives. That is, until its exposure—when old ways shed by earlier repentance are found to have somehow returned. If so, the discovering need not be defeating. It can become a *hope*—a call signaling the Holy Spirit's readiness to bring us *more* than *back*—a readiness to lead us *forward!*

It's His way of offering a new day—one calling for yet-again-new wineskins. I say, let's receive this from the Holy Spirit. But for my soul, at least, I must remember that all old wine-skins were new, once. My having received the "new" at any other time than today holds the portent of danger. It's embarrassing to have new wine explode all over you because you didn't recognize how old your once-new wineskins had become. I know—and I've told you about it.

Still, we serve a Savior who not only forgives sin such as mine, but who also delights to renew—again and again. My "stumbling" report is related in case it just might freshly equip others for a new season of His grace. The new wine is flowing today. New wineskins are all that can contain it.

Jack Hayford, "When New Wineskins Start to Age," *Ministries Today* (September/October 1992): 24–25.

The Leader's Edge

The brilliant capacities of the human mind are a gift of God never to be devalued or disdained, yet by Western man's values, the equally worthy capacities of the human emotions consistently are devalued and disdained. The proper place of *passion* in a leader's thought and practice is essential to avoiding the sterility of a merely cerebral approach to grand issues. Let wise leaders lead with passion—in their personal life where God wholly endorses and welcomes our warmly passionate pursuit of His life, His love and the fullness of His Spirit; and in their public life where emotion is only suspect if it betrays selfishness, small-heartedness or manipulative intent. Purified passion seen in a leader cannot be justly accused as manipulation. A leader only "manipulates" when he seeks to get people to do what he wants them to do for *his* best interests—a leader "leads" when he seeks to get people to do what is best for *theirs*. Passion is worthy in such leadership.

For More...

The Passion for Fullness is a book themed by the message I brought at the Lausanne Congress on Evangelism, convened via Billy Graham's influence in Manila, Philippines in 1989.[4] Its message has been welcomed in all quarters of Christian tradition, exemplified by the generous affirmation of James Robison, born of Southern Baptist tradition, who described it as "one of the four books that have most influenced my life."

[chapter 6] Concerning "Less Patient About 'Less Passion'"

I was conversing with a young pastor from Michigan as we sat at breakfast together. He was one of forty-five who were with me that week for one of the "Consultations" I conduct with a different group each month. Over twelve hundred participants have come from more than forty denominations since I recently began this weeklong, personally interactive opportunity for senior pastors who feel it worth their while to have me share with them. Besides focusing on God's Word, I interface with them at length on the issues of pastoral leadership.

Over breakfast, this bright, gifted leader was "picking my brain." "Pastor Jack," he prodded, "what is your most compelling goal right now?"

I thought of a dozen or more: to walk with Jesus in faith and purity; to love Anna as a devoted husband; to minister God's Word with power wherever I go; to serve the staff and family at The Church On The Way in any way I'm asked; to build The King's College and Seminary library; to advance

Living Way Ministries; to give time to the five writing projects I'm engaged in currently; to help each viewer-listener of our radio-television broadcast—and the list goes on.

I Didn't Say Any of Those

But I listed none of those goals, because I knew where he really wanted the conversation to go. He was actually asking, "Can you help me target the values, patterns and approaches to leadership that will help me become a more fruitful pastor?"

Like most of us, he was looking for something *tangible*—a *plan* or a *system*...something to "make things work better." And while I know plans, organization and administration are essential, I also knew he had plenty of that. That's why I said, "You know, Chuck, a lot of things are important—but for me, *everything* finally resolves around these two issues:

- [■] **Worshiping God and heeding His Word...***with passion;* **and**
- [■] **Walking with God in the fullness of His Spirit...***with passion.***"**

In expressing this, I strongly emphasized the words *with passion,* not because I was impatient with Chuck but because I am becoming less and less patient with an idea— with *a spirit*—I seem to encounter increasingly today.

There is everything from a low-grade rumble creating suspicion to an outright prohibition afoot toward passionate faith, passionate leadership, passionate worship or a passionate pulpit. But let me take issue—maybe you will agree with me. *There are times that passion ought to preempt patience.*

I'm not only referencing the studied social reserve or near-smug coolness pastoral professionalism might induce. More so, I'm talking about the reduced boldness to *lead* as a leader's "passion" is critiqued by observers as being "manipulation." The earnest-hearted leader who faces such criticism often relents for fear of appearing superficial or self-promoting.

I'm talking about the doctrinaire confusion parading as "the mystery of God's sovereignty," which suggests that any passionate pursuit of God's promises is merely humanistic. I'm talking about the branding of outwardly verbal, physically expressive worship as *Charismatic* rather than as *scriptural,* with the suggestion that silence is more reverent than a shout. As I move among church leaders by the thousands, engaging hundreds regularly in personal conversation, I am bumping into what I want to brand *a spirit of intimidation.*

While I am anything but a wild-eyed fanatic, and would never argue for emotional indulgence as anyone's "right" nor for emotionalism as the believer's "liberty in the Spirit," I want to argue a case for renewed and released passion—especially among us who lead.

A Discerning Distinction

First, this is no plea for passion as a carnal indulgence, or for anger retitled "holy zeal" when people or things don't suit us. We have all seen more than enough of that shallow, selfish "pushiness" of the flesh erupting when people use passion to "get things done my way...*NOW!*" So my loss of patience is not the sulking criticism or glaring fury of someone wanting to enthrone impatience or to license passion on any terms. But an irresistible law of diminishing return, which isn't as righteous as some think, can be observed:

1. **When *passivity* toward a trying circumstance is defined as *patience*, and spiritual opposition is unidentified or power-prayer unengaged.**

2. **Or worse, when the doctrine of divine sovereignty is invoked over tragedy, and a *faith* that is actually *fatalism* manifests in the sloth born of spiritual ignorance.**

For example, setbacks, pain or discouragement can easily

lean a person's soul toward the weariness that a long trial or undiscerned demonic assault can produce. A lying whisper may suggest "patient endurance," when instead it's time we rose with a *passionate heartcry to the Father.* It's very possible that something you are facing right now calls for *passion,* not *patience.*

Restudy the Psalms! Frequent cases of complaint to the Almighty are registered there, and they were written with the passion of a songwriter! Too easily, even while encouraging others to "stand in faith," a beleaguered leader may succumb to a stance of prostrating himself before a trial rather than resisting a satanically disguised ruse. Don't cave in to difficulties when the option of victory in Christ is always ours! "Thanks be unto God, which always causeth us to triumph in Christ" (2 Cor. 2:14, KJV).

With this, I am not defining *triumph* as a trial-free life. Neither am I telling you every victory is untinged by the blood of battle or will be garnered without pain. But I am saying that victory is possessed by the passionate. It isn't served up on a plate of predestination that bypasses the process of faith's partnership with God's mightiness.

Let's resist the subtlety of any voice that argues that we

were called to sire a new strain of "the stiff-upper-lipped"—a supposed new nobility who bow silently before present circumstances rather than rising to intercede and letting the fire of trial stoke the passion of their intercession. "The Spirit also helps in our weaknesses...the Spirit Himself makes intercession for us with groanings which cannot be uttered" (Rom. 8:26). That's passion applied as directed by the mightiest single doctrinal resource afforded us in the Scriptures—the Epistle to the Romans.

There is no way to separate the believer's response to the Holy Spirit's call to His brand of energized intercessory prayer from the promise of becoming "more than conquerors through Him who loved us" (cf. Rom. 8:26–27 and 8:37–39). The whole passage breathes of a passion that never intended to have a *creed* substituted for a *cry.* Religiousness dictates that believers surrender to circumstances and call it "trust," but God's Word calls believers to surrender to Him and to expect His hand to uphold, move in and bring His victory. "Through God we will do valiantly, for it is He who shall tread down our enemies" (Ps. 108:13).

There Is a "Divine Discontent"

In other words, I'm wanting to discern and overcome that

so-called "patience" that submits to the subtlety of human fear, doubt, passivity or pride, that lying voice that whispers, "Don't get too excited about God or expect too much of Him. Tough it out—*be patient.*" Because, in fact, the Bible reveals there *are* times when a *divine discontent* needs to motivate me—not a *patient passivity.*

- Passion, not patience, moved Jesus through Gethsemane's ordeal and paved the way to Calvary. (See Luke 22:39-46.)
- Passion, not patience, brought spiritual breakthrough when effort was made to silence the church. (See Acts 4:23-31.)
- Passion, not patience, brought Paul to discover "grace sufficient" for the satanic battle he was waging. (See 2 Corinthians 12:7-10.)

There are many other biblical examples of pure passion in the face of adversity. Even Job didn't take his agony lying down. His body's posture may have been prostrated by trial and his patience boiled to a refined purity, but he consistently made his appeal to God. Even though He failed to discern that Satan—not God—was the source of his trouble, he still cried out in faith with a passion that distills in some of the most victorious utterances in God's Word:

Though He slay me, yet will I trust Him.

—Job 13:15

He knows the way that I take; when He has tested me, I shall come forth as gold.

—Job 23:10

I know that my Redeemer lives...that in my flesh I shall see God.

—Job 19:25–26

Let Me Encourage You

Whatever you're going through...whatever your personal challenge...whatever your family trials...whatever your economic circumstances...whatever your physical pain... whatever your wearied soul's tiredness—please engage a partnership. Partner with me as a fellow warrior committed to *passionately pursue God's promises as a life principle.* Don't allow human concoctions of supposed doctrinal superiority to argue, intimidate or intellectualize you into a corner of passivity. God's sovereignty is a grand reality, and His almightiness and ultimate control in the universe is unquestioned. But God's promises to humankind are not automatic in application—they are for those who actively pursue them and who passionately receive and abide in the love they reveal.

You will seek Me and find Me, when you search for Me with all your heart.

—JEREMIAH 29:13

Take time to examine a few more such calls to passion:

- [■] *To know God* in the riches of His wisdom (Prov. 8:17)
- [■] *To worship God* in the most threatening of circumstances (Ps. 63:1–8)
- [■] *To approach God* with boldness of faith (Matt. 7:7–8)
- [■] *To believe God* is totally and favorably disposed toward your need, your hunger or your heart-quest for His Holy Spirit's fullness (Luke 11:5–13)

Just as the word *passion* was central to my response with that young pastor, my words evoke passion as I write to you. Decades of leading and teaching God's people are producing this net result: I am certain that *cool Christianity* will never succeed in resisting the bonfires of unbelief that intimidate souls, nor the fiery darts of evil assault that rain from today's skies. You have to fight fire with fire!

Don't be afraid to let God's Holy Spirit ignite you!

Jack Hayford, "I'm Losing My Patience," *Ministries Today* (May/June 2001): 18–19.

The Leader's Edge

Aristotle said, "The unexamined life is not worth living." The New Testament says, "Let a man examine himself" (1 Cor. 11:28), while in the Psalms, David says, "Search me...know my heart...try me" (Ps. 139:23). This article is among several sown throughout these pages to press leaders to probe deeply, honestly and with a readiness to receive possible refreshing or renewal in those principles that make leadership durable and enduring.

For More...

Consider reading Eugene Peterson's *A Long Obedience in the Same Direction*.[5] Online resources for pastors and spiritual leaders are also available at www.jackhayford.com.

[chapter 7] Prescription for a Timeless Ministry

MARTIN Luther pressed the point that if we're not at the foremost edge of the spiritual struggle, we're really not in the battle at all.

All of us want to be on the cutting edge. I know I do. That's why I struggled so intensely during a time of great physical pain and bewilderment. I wondered if I would simply become a worn-out relic or be an able recruit for the move of the Holy Spirit today.

During those days of personal struggle I began to receive fresh lessons from the Lord. I was reminded that while cultures, methods and technologies change, the key to touching people timelessly for eternity has not changed. Ultimately it is done in living out "the basics."

The Holy Spirit gave me God's timeless promise from Isaiah 11: "In that day…the Lord shall set His hand again *the second time…*" (v. 11, emphasis added). While meditating on that prophetic statement, these words came: "Stand fast in faithfulness! You will be a participant in what I am about to do."

I knew this word was for all who will accept the ingredients of a *timeless ministry*—one always available to God's timeless principles. Touched by this hope, I sought guidelines for "a second time" visitation. Ten timeless principles distilled:

1. Pursue an Intimate Walk With God

The Bible uses the word *know,* as in "Adam knew Eve his wife," to mean more than "acquaintance"—it signifies the intimate experience of a husband and wife during intercourse. The human figure of sexual union as analogous to a spiritual relationship with God can sound mystical, but it helps me hear God's call to press toward Him—to know Him. Such passion can lead to a new intimacy with Jesus. From our interchange of life while with Him, His Word-life seed is sown in us, guaranteeing revealed insight and spiritual fruitfulness.

2. Target a Life With Design and Discipline

God told Moses, "See to it that you make them according to

the pattern which was shown you" (Exod. 25:40). Without designs for life—direction born of the Spirit—serving becomes hit-or-miss. Dreams and visions—God's heaven-born designs—are promised to the Spirit-filled saint.

However, we also need to observe disciplines that are clearly enunciated in His Word. Without designs *and* disciplines, we become either visionaries who gain dreams from God yet aimlessly chase them, or legalists who know biblical guidelines but live them antiseptically, unintegrated with the life-giving Spirit who gave them. The divinely targeted life seeks the *way* of the Lord revealed by the Spirit in prayer and obeys the *will* of the Lord as revealed in His Word.

3. Commit to Cultivating Body Ministry

Ephesians 4:11 names the five office ministries, not so much to identify them as to underscore their purpose: to release the people of God into liberty, wholeness and effective ministry. Those we serve, like Gideon, tend to see themselves as unworthy of ministry potential. We must see them as God saw Gideon and serve them as potential "mighty ones of valor." As we pour out our lives to lovingly shepherd God's people, they will begin to see themselves as God sees them—anointed people of His kingdom, filled with the wealth of heaven and capacitated for greatness in Christ.

4. Seek *Faith-fully* to Build Marriages and Families

I hyphenate the word *faith-fully* because I believe the Holy Spirit is calling every one of us who lead to gain a faith-filled conviction about our society. *God isn't done with it yet!* The Spirit's power can redeem the family as an institution again. He can raise new models to gloriously assert the family's value and place before the eyes of a watching world. We need to hear and believe God's call to "faith-fully" expect and pursue the recovering and rebuilding of our families.

5. Respond Passionately to God's Love for the Lost

John died when his car was smashed on the freeway. However, only three months before, John had received Jesus when one of my pastor-friends led him to Christ as the first convert in his new pastorate!

I wept when I heard that story, somehow reminded of the preciousness of each individual soul and the eternal loss that unchangingly abides as the horrible option to salvation. That one soul rekindled a passionate response in my soul. Does yours need to be refired in any way?

6. Walk an Unswerving Pathway of Integrity

Answering a call to integrity must be more than just an emotional reaction to failures we hear of too often among leaders. We need a personal, practical recognition of the necessity for total accountability in the everyday matters of our leadership. For example:

- What words and style do we employ publicly—even when we're simply announcing coming events in our churches? Are we flamboyant and promotionalistic? Or are we forthright, simple and informative?
- What dimension of integrity governs our choice of means for personal relaxation? What supplies our entertainment?
- How do we handle the temptation to manipulate relationships to get what we want from people?
- In private, do we still hear the voice of the Spirit correcting and adjusting us?

7. Keep an Unabashed Openness to Supernatural Ministry

The Lord calls us to do more than just accept a *doctrine* of supernatural ministry—He calls us to the risks of its *dynamic*—to live in constant availability to His miracle presence. I object to the pious but misguided idea that God expects us to believe He will sprinkle miracles like diamonds everywhere we go. But He *does* call us to be people of miracle expectancy—people of power, moving wholeheartedly in whatever manifestations of His Spirit He gives.

We need fresh fullness in every encounter and circumstance lest we be dulled to function merely in holy habits without holy power. We must face down the cowardice in us that always opts for the path of small demand on our faith. The road to supernatural ministry is neither neat nor fun. A too tightly packed program is not liable to experience the truly exceptional works of the Spirit. Neither is sensationalism to be equated with true supernatural vitality.

8. Respond to the Great Commission

For effective worldwide missions, we need a blending of

twenty-first-century contemporaneity with first-century enthusiasm. In my youth and early ministry, missions conferences—replete with flags, artifacts, goal boards and faith-promise cards—were everywhere. I became "burned out" on such fanfare and determined not to use those means anymore. I don't know if those same approaches would work today, anyway. But I do know this: The Lord is calling us to stir our congregations to vibrant action and participation in world missions.

We need fresh strategies and a new, truly sacrificial approach to budgeting for our intensified outreach to the world. Just as the Holy Spirit raised up vital missions' visionaries to shake the church in past generations, He is awakening us today.

9. Demonstrate a Biblical Sensitivity to the Spirit of Prophecy

The Holy Spirit is always speaking to urge us to listen with fresh vitality. We face a high challenge to keep our ears tuned to His voice. At the same time, there is the need for fresh discernment and a deeper look into the eternal Word to keep everything in perspective. A measure of excitement over prophecy is valid, but a significant part of today's glibness and glitz is under question. Discernment *is* truly needed, but still let us *never* despise prophesyings. Let's ground them all in the timeless security found in committing to our last principle:

10. Do Everything on the Unshakable Bedrock of the Scriptures

The promise of Isaiah 11:11, which so stirred my soul, is available to all of us. "A second time" is a summons for us to be part of a new visitation. The Lord recurrently fulfills prophetic Scripture in multiple ways. Just as He fulfilled Isaiah's prophecy six centuries before Christ by regathering Israel after its exile, He has fulfilled it again in the twentieth century by gathering the Jews in modern-day Israel. And He is *still* fulfilling His Word, always ready to pour out grace wherever He can find people who will hear His voice and respond.

Jack Hayford, "Prescription for a Timeless Ministry," *Ministries Today* (May/June 1990): 48; Jack Hayford, "Prescription for a Timeless Ministry (Part II)," *Ministries Today* (September/October 1990): 32–33.

The Leader's Edge

I have concluded this section with my report of a "personal summons" to prepare for a year when global focus was on Y2K's highest hopes, grandest excitement, direst threats, all mixed with miscellaneous *millennial glitz*. What seemed to be a time for "commencement"—leaping toward tomorrow's opportunities—I found to reveal more the need for "further prep school" if the future's deepest possibilities were to be realized. It is probably a *constant* axiom for the sensible, sensitive leader's consideration: *Resist opportunism*—God's purposes in your life are never "in a hurry"—*Be patient in preparation*—God's wisdom and power distill upon those who "wait for Him."

For More...

John Maxwell's gift to leaders is the substance of decades of discovery in his own journey. His books and other resources are abundant and available through INJOY Group website at www.injoy.com. Or you may contact them at The INJOY Group, 4725 River Green Pkwy., Duluth, GA 30096. Their phone number is (800) 333-6506.

[chapter 8] Preparation for "Kingdom" Influence

MOST of us can still remember when the Y2K phantom dissipated like ground fog before high noon. The prognostications of unspeakable horror proved invalid, and for a moment it was tempting for some to mock the millennium fearmongers. For my part, however, I was already into a pursuit of applying a sensitive, practical response to the Holy Spirit's earlier dealings with me.

Without pretending to have had great foresight on my part, in the weeks counting down to that now-past but very memorable opening of the new millennium, I heard Him calling me to a year of preparation. While that time of the Spirit's dealing with my own heart is a pair of years behind us now, the message—very applicable to my present experience then—seems timeless to me in principle. Let me share it with you, because *anytime* is a wise time for prepping ourselves for God's next season in our souls.

It was an early morning, November 1999, when at my

morning devotions I was strongly impressed with the words, "This shall be a year of preparation to you." Simultaneously, without conscious analysis, but with a sense of "directedness," that inner constraint I identify as the Lord's prompting stirred me to turn to the Book of Esther. As I turned the pages of my Bible, I remembered that she had received a similar assignment—an appointment to "twelve months' preparation" (Esther 2:12). Further examination of the context *riveted* my attention on a striking detail: "Seven choice maidservants were provided for her [Esther] from the king's palace" (v. 9).

Without laboring to be clever or creative, and with concern that I not violate the true sense of the textual setting, I began to muse over the likely implications of these words in Esther's situation. Upon prayerful reflection I drew a pair of conclusions:

- These seven "choice" women commissioned to assist the preparation of a candidate for queen would have been skilled, sensitive and wise in the practical issues of palace life and the expectations of potential royalty.
- The fact that there were "seven" suggests a variety of skills and experience, so that each woman would be making a distinct contribution to Esther's yearlong "preparation" (v. 12).

I knew of nowhere to turn to verify all the results of my further consideration, but it seems reasonable that this "preparation team" would have focused on obvious areas of appropriate care, instruction and training, such as:

1. **Cleansing—for physical purification and confirmation of absence of infection or disease before coming to the king**

2. **Beautification—noted in verse 12, which would incorporate physical conditioning as well as beauty treatments**

3. **Nutrition—to assure her dietary habits conformed to the court, and to secure her health for her mission**

4. **Regimen—to familiarize her with the schedule and events that constitute palace life**

5. **Training—to tune her understanding to palace protocols and prevent an embarrassing (or even fatal) faux pas**

6. **Wisdom—to enable her ability to communicate sensibly and intelligently**

7. **Companionship—seeing as this virgin maiden would be ushered into the king's presence for lovemaking as well as a prospective bride and lifetime partner**

Pictures of the Holy Spirit?

These seven "choice maidservants" had one task—to prepare Esther for what became her God-ordained destiny.

This fact moved me to wonder if "a year of preparation" would do all of us good—shaping us under the Holy Spirit's workings in our lives for His inauguration of whatever our King may have in mind for our future. It seemed worthy of writing what so strongly spoke to me, for irrespective of *when* any transition or opportunity may rise before any of us, "being prepared" for the King's purposes is always a worthy agenda to guide our thoughts, lifestyle and focus.

Just as there were "seven choice maidservants" assigned to assist Esther's preparation, I thought of several passages in the Word that describe the Spirit's ministry in "sevens." For example, Isaiah 11:2; Zechariah 4:1–10 and Revelation 4:5, taken together, seem to reference distinctive facets of His Person and work—freeing us, enabling us and purifying us. So it was, without laboring to force these texts or my thoughts regarding the seven maidservants provided to prepare Esther, that I was personally moved to invite the Holy Spirit to work in my life in seven distinct ways as I approached the new year.

My reasoning deepened my readiness to respond to His prompting, for no matter what season or year we face, a prophetic mood and mind-set is appropriate. God is always "up to something," and He is always looking for servants who are ready to meet the moment with hearts, minds and lives that can move in partnership with His will and way for their world. That prophetic viewpoint is what has motivated my personal passion to answer the call to a year of preparation, and in the seven ideas noted above I saw seven ways I—or any of us—can welcome the Holy Spirit to move in and upon us—preparing us for God's "next big thing"— whether in our world or simply in our private life.

Here are seven parallels to the likely efforts of Esther's seven maidens, practical applications of spiritual principles the Holy Spirit might well work in any one of us to ready us for action "in the King's court":

1. **Cleansing: "Who shall ascend into the hill of the Lord? or who shall stand in his holy place? He that hath clean hands, and a pure heart...He shall receive the blessing from the Lord" (Ps. 24:3–5, KJV). Openness to the Holy Spirit's dealings about purity of heart and life is a pivotal issue when pursuing blessing.**

2. **Beautification: The life that is a "sweet-smelling aroma" is unselfishly sacrificing and servant-oriented (Phil. 4:18). The "beautiful feet" of Isaiah 52:7 reveal a pace-setting lifestyle of spreading God's love, peace and forgiveness. "Lord, I pray, help me toward a more consistent witness for Jesus and toward a deepened *servant-heartedness* toward people."**

3. **Nutrition: Besides the biblical dietary directive I'll**

mention below, let me affirm and repeat a "trumpet call" I am hearing everywhere throughout today's church: The Holy Spirit has issued at least one "nutritional condition" regarding revival. He is calling us to seek God and call upon Him with fasting and prayer, which have always been prerequisites to spiritual breakthrough. (See Isaiah 58:6-14.)

4. Regimen: Besides my refusal to miss the Spirit's call to "God's chosen fast," I would do well to reassess my personal maintenance of the "temple" of my own body by being renewed in plain, everyday dietary good judgment. Fornication isn't the only way that our "temple" may be polluted. (See 1 Corinthians 6:19-20.) Maybe the Lord does care more than we may think about carnal indulgence and the world-minded spirit of gluttony.

5. Training: There is an appropriate "court behavior" for sons and daughters of the King of heaven. It involves disciplines that are beyond religious systems and requires growth in relational sensitivity. Jesus made clear that it is vain to attempt to access God's best if we haven't sought first to resolve the worst in our relationships. (See Matthew 5:23-24.) Who knows what revival breakthrough simply awaits healing of relationships between me and some other party?

6. Wisdom: I've entered into a new-dimensioned covenant with the Lord this year, a commitment to spend more disciplined time in His Word—diligently, thoughtfully and prayerfully. The prayer in Psalm 119:18 for "opened eyes" to behold the wonders of

God's Word may well be the pathway to seeing increased signs and wonders of His Word at work!

7. **Companionship:** It is a delicate subject to investigate what may have been the schooling Esther received regarding her role as the king's "beloved." However, one thing is sure: As surely as she would have been purified as a virginal bride, she would nonetheless have been taught how to be a passionate one. It's enough for me to simply be reminded—the Holy Spirit's call to loving and passionate worship and adoration of the King is lifelong. It calls us away from conformity to the sophistication of the world's style-consciousness to a transforming that opens the way to the release of God's will in, through and around my life. (See Romans 12:1-2.)

Consider the implications of those features of possible preparation. It doesn't take a new year to prompt a response. It simply underscores the timeless call to always "be ready—*prepared*—in season and out of season."

Jack Hayford, "Fizz, Fear and Frustration," *Ministries Today* (March/April): 18–19.

Section 2
The Penetrating Edge

The Leader's Pathway to Power

Power in any arena is usually the decisive "edge," determining what goals are reached, tasks completed, victories gained, successes tabulated. Power comes in many different packages—money, political influence, information, superior assets, animal magnetism or human dynamism. There is one power supply that, if pursued at all, is too often a source of last resort.

I am privileged to know leaders in most fields— from business to education, from politics to the military, from entertainment to church life. In every realm there are those who will rise to affirm the truth of the timeless prophecy: "'Not by might nor by power, but by My Spirit,' says the LORD" (Zech. 4:6). Beyond human energy and resource, the power that penetrates life circumstances with the deepest, fullest, most fruitful and transforming mightiness comes by one means before and beyond all—*prayer.*

These seven articles span the power of prayer from the privilege of intimacy with God to the awesomeness of being invited to partner with Him in determining global issues.

The Leader's Edge

The infusion of the dynamic of a healthy prayer gathering of people who believe God is not only alive, but also *interested*, is more than inspiring. It is igniting—lighting a fire of faith that has greater penetrating power on life circumstances than a welder's cutting torch on sheet metal. We open this section with the leader's *call* to prayer—not only to participate in prayer gatherings, but also to cultivate and lead them.

For More...

"Where can I find 'more'...more I can teach as I lead?" That was my personal cry when I made the determination that the midweek gathering will be a distinctly targeted revisiting of New Testament prayer power, not a potpourri of religious options for a handful who visit. My findings resulted in *Prayer Is Invading the Impossible*, published by Bridge. Now in its "umpteenth" printing, this study of the riches and depth contained in the multiple facets of prayer (such as "supplication" [*deesis*], and "intercession" [*entunchano*]) has been testified to as having "forever altered my thinking about prayer" for innumerable believers.

[chapter 9]

Gathered for "Great Grace"

I'VE just come from our midweek prayer meeting, and colloquially speaking, I'm *hyped!* It was Book of Acts fare, and though I had already planned to write you about the place of *prayer meeting* in the local church, I hadn't expected this evening's *movement.* Now my approach is all the more impassioned, coming in the wake of the enthusiasm (that is, *God fullness*) and blessing (that is, *glory presence*) overflowing me via tonight's powerhouse meeting.

Maybe the Holy Spirit arranged this setup. That's conceivable, since it isn't my nature to "puff" things or to approach them with a rush. But enthusiasm for prayer meeting does need rekindling for some of us. Without question, for some the event needs a resurrection from its earlier reputation, with lingering memories of lifelessness and tired formalities. Many of us experienced midweek services that died long before they were buried, and it's enough to discourage some from ever trying again.

The memory of rigor-mortised prayer meetings isn't easily dismissed. I wonder how many leaders hesitate to initiate a weekly corporate prayer meeting because images of spiritual death still haunt them—quavering voices mouthing platitudinous petitions worded the same way week after week; clichéd prayer requests, from "Let's remember the missionaries," to "Let's not forget our unsaved loved ones." It's a ghostly picture enough to "spook" anyone away from a vision of life-giving possibilities.

The Missing Meeting

Prayer meetings are harder than ever to find today, even on the schedule of a "renewal" church. In noting this, I risk sounding snobbishly superior or arrogantly condescending (especially having already asserted that we have a great one at our church). But, dear pastor/leader, I'm not here to pulpit-pound on prayer, and neither am I here to condemn, nor will I strut. But I would like to probe. I would like to ask some questions, which, if answered practically, seem to me to indicate the absolute necessity of a weekly assembly of believers willing to bear the issue of the local church's prayer mission on their shoulders—or better yet, on their knees.

1. **When can a congregation ever kneel together? For very long?**

2. **What opportunity for focused intercession does a church family need to answer the biblical priority of this ministry? How regular should it be?**

3. **What issues are *not* pursued in prayer, for want of adequate time to give them definition so that sensible, discerning supplication can be made?**

4. **When can regular biblical instruction on intercession be provided in order to stimulate and guide the congregation to a lifestyle of prayer? And fasting?**

Well-Meaning Objections

I'm fully sympathetic with the problems that can hinder the pastor who wants, but finds it difficult to foster and maintain, a vital prayer meeting. People are busier today than ever. School kids need to get to bed early, and that keeps families home. Bad experiences with past church traditions neutralize vision. Passivity and indifference prevail. But despite the difficulties, the Book of Acts calls us to build a church of prayer-meeting participants.

Apparently, certain things happen only when a strongly representative group seeks God—when corporate, concerted prayer is the primary agenda instead of teaching, study times or other valuable facets of church experience.

Consider that:

- [■] The church was birthed in a prayer meeting. "These all continued with one accord" (Acts 1:14). Pentecost was the answer to their obedient waiting on God. (See Luke 24:49.)

- [■] The early Christians forged a way of life involving regular prayer gatherings as well as assemblies for fellowship, teaching and other purposes. (See Acts 2:42.)

- [■] The prayer meeting that caused the "holy shake-up" recorded in Acts 4:23–31 was a gathering in which, as a group, they "raised their voice to God" (v. 24). It wasn't just a praise gathering—this group of people poured out their hearts to the Lord *unto breakthrough*. Because of their depth of concern and conviction of faith, they prayed with a passion that exceeded a more socially appropriate, conversational tone.

Intercessory Mission

It isn't that such prayer meetings can't take place on Sunday mornings, but simply that they generally don't. Nor do I think they necessarily should. Sunday's worship service elements are pretty well dictated by the edificational needs of believers—uplifting praise, invigorating fellowship, unburdening prayer, edifying teaching, liberating worship. These are the basics of weekly spiritual nurture. Virtually any congregation's valid Sunday morning inspirational and instructional agenda just doesn't allow time for the inter-cessory mission of the church.

Time for Warfare

Of course, prayers are a part of any Christian gathering, but there is a vast difference between "sharing a burden" in prayer and "engaging prayer's warfare." For intercessory prayer to be focused and pursued, it takes time to analyze an issue, to determine prayer's direction and then to attack with extended prayer. Effective intercession must identify the target together before "striking" it in faith. The energy released through corporate, Holy Spirit-enabled interces-sion doesn't conjure through "excitement," but through *examination* (unitedly seeing the issue) and *exegesis* (joining it to the promises in God's Word). Both take time, and that's what "prayer meeting" is about.

Reinstitution of the congregational prayer meeting is as desir-able as it is essential. When Paul says in 1 Timothy 2:1–2, "I exhort first of all that supplications, prayers, intercessions, and giving of thanks be made for all men, for kings and all who are in authority, that we may lead a quiet and peaceable life," the result of such prayer action by the church is beauti-fully explained—a happier and more peaceful society, better towns, cities and nations. The praying church decides whether this will take place or not, but it will require more than prayer "in passing."

Supplication (*deesis*) and intercession (*entunchano*) are intense expressions in the Greek, as any study of the words will reveal. They are forms of prayer that cannot be exercised apart from three things:

- [■] **Time—to define what is being implored of God's kingdom.**
- [■] **Unity—which only rises when teaching and discussion homogenizes hearts unto agreement.**
- [■] **Passion—which truth may generate, but leadership models and releases through bold, open, declarative prayer.**

It is by these means that a congregation is moved to bond in faith that God is hearing and that He will answer. These are essential elements to birthing the prayer passion that will grip a local body and move them forward in prayer—their objective clear and their faith confirmed that they are "gathered for power"—gathered to make a difference!

I know, of course, that the volume of our prayers, the multiplying of our words and the extent of our weeping do not *earn* answers from God. But experience does show that when prayer is filled with passion, something *burns*—something is ignited of prayer's potential to bring breakthrough, release, healing and transformation.

The Coming Revival

There are prophecies going forth today that say America can yet be saved as a nation—that she might continue to be a base from which gospel life and light may emanate throughout the world. They prophesy that her homes might be whole again, that multitudes of people might be born again into the kingdom of God. No one in his right mind believes that America deserves such grace or that such a visitation would save everyone. But there is still a merciful call of the Spirit—"If My people"—and it's never been rescinded (2 Chron. 7:14). Now the possession of such possibilities in prayer waits to be gained through the travail of praying congregations.

But that's only one reason for the newly awakened prayer thrust and the renewal of the prayer meeting in the body of Christ. There's another. More and more sensitive, Spirit-filled believers are attesting to a sense that we are on the edge of something new from heaven, that God is "in the wings," waiting to step onto the stage of global history and display His power in unprecedented dimensions. I'm one of those believers, and maybe you are, too.

But with this hope there's one thing we can't escape: Only prayer brings a greater experiencing of the kingdom. That's why Jesus taught us to pray for the kingdom's entry into our world scene. He called us to pray because by prayer *alone*—it's the *sole* means—will God's kingdom purposes "come" into our world. That's what "Thy kingdom come" is talking about!

John Wesley said, "God does nothing except in answer to believing prayer." To which Derek Prince has added, "In honor of His Son, who died to redeem His Church, God will do nothing on earth by any other means than through His Church's prayer." It is the church at prayer that opens prison doors (Acts 12:5-19) and realizes God's direction for kingdom expansion (Acts 13:1-3). Those two instances are, by themselves, sufficient to point us to our knees and to lift our faith with expectancy for today's "prison doors" to be opened and today's God's "kingdom" boundaries to be expanded. That evidence in His Word may not be exhaustive, but it is conclusive—and abundantly sufficient to warrant our answering a new trumpet call today.

Jack Hayford, "Gathered for Power," *Ministries Today* (November/December 1994): 6–7.

The Leader's Edge

When Bill Clinton was president of the United States, the outcry of resentment among a host of evangelical Christians continued throughout his two terms. I instituted a policy of prayer, convinced a watershed moment had arrived for the church in America. Either we would complain over moral lassitude, or we would intercede for divine grace and protection over the leader God's providence had brought into office (Rom. 13:1). This pair of articles define what some "heard" of the Scripture's call—a call that still resounds and that must ever and always be heard if a "peaceable life" is to be known in this or any nation (1 Tim. 2:1-3).[6]

For More...

Local prayer groups may be enriched in study by using *Kingdom Warfare*, one of the *Kingdom Life Study Guides* produced by Thomas Nelson. Also available are two audio study series from Living Way Ministries, "New Waves Of Intercession" and "Refining Our Focus." Both are representative teachings on intercession brought at The Church On The Way.

[chapter 10]

To Set the Course of a Nation

AS we brink the inauguration of our forty-second president of the United States, a peculiar and demanding challenge lies before pastoral leadership. It's *peculiar* because it's disturbing to find so many of God's people in spiritual gridlock over the election of Bill Clinton. And it's *demanding* because we'll prove less than accountable to our shepherd-office if we allow our flocks to stray from a biblical view of the church's (and thereby each believer's) mission amid the world's political milieu.

To serve God's sheep with fidelity, like it or not, I have to face up to a dual pastoral assignment at this time:

1. **To nurture people beyond temporal dismay, such as many felt over the past election.**

2. **To call my congregation to a true spirit of prayer for Bill Clinton—our nation's newly assigned leader.**

While it's hard to tell by the reaction of some Christians, God didn't lose this election. He wasn't even running! And whatever consternation may justifiably be felt over this election's confirmation of the moral drift in our society, it's ludicrous to ever suppose that any one party or person's control of government is the hope for securing our nation's moral ground. Morality has never been the product of group legislation. Now as ever, it is only achieved by personal transformation—and those possibilities only transmit when the church functions as the church and not as a political auxiliary dependent upon its government's support or approval.

Many Christians have apparently been lulled into a spiritual stupor by recent tendencies in parts of today's church, bound by the notion that the politics of the land either constitute or command the church's agenda. Such Christians have fallen prey to lost discernment, failing to distinguish between two activities—both righteous:

1. **Seeking to employ the privileges of a free society by using personal and political influence toward the maximum good in the light of God's truth.**
2. **Recognizing that whatever the outcome of those efforts, the church's ultimate mission transcends those activities—and our attitudes must, also.**

Now, I heartily applaud the efforts of all fellow Christians who involve themselves in the political process, seeking to be salt and light in every way and every place they can. In fact, I'm pastor to some highly placed personalities and a sizable number of government employees. But I'm committed to helping everyone whom I lead to distinguish between the believer's call to penetrate the political system as *light* and the desire to seek to control it by *power.*

A New Initiative

This January [1993] is the time for us to call our people to rise as the servants of the living God, to love the people and leaders of our land and to earnestly, graciously pray for them. It's time to seize a new initiative unlimited by political agendas and lead our flocks to a clear perspective on the New Testament's call to impact society by love and good works (1 Pet. 2:11–17).

This is an hour for biblical citizenship, not political Pharisaism; for loving, not lamentation. We must cease passing judgment (which is God's business) and recommit to a spirit of love for our national family. After all, our mission isn't to correct a culture by gaining control of it, but to "shine as lights in the midst of a crooked and perverse nation" (Phil. 2:14–16; Matt. 5:11–16). To the exact degree I embrace disdain for anyone or any attribute characterizing the world around me, I become neutralized for ministering the loving, merciful, delivering gospel of God to it.

On the day Bill Clinton takes the oath of office, by God's grace may every spiritual leader in this land kneel before God with the discernment to function as spiritual supporters of our president. God's call to spiritually undergird a nation's leaders is essentially unrelated to any feelings we have of political or moral disagreement. Our pastoral task includes leading our people to see the difference.

At the risk of appearing disgustingly religious or politically naive, I want to propose that on Inauguration Day we lead our people to rise up in prayer and thanksgiving to God—for freedom for all those being placed in office.

Why Be Thankful?

1. Be thankful because of the revelation in God's Word regarding how leaders ascend to office.

Psalm 75:1-10 is a pointed statement attributing all promotion to the sovereign God. "Exaltation [promotion, political power] comes neither from the east nor from the west nor from the south. But God is the Judge: He puts down one, and exalts another" (vv. 6-7). Though the Lord didn't ask our consent to place President-elect Clinton in the White House, He has commanded our prayers for Him.

Let's assure our people that God isn't nervous about the winds and whims of human political enterprise. He's the almighty Lord and Judge amid and above them! "The authorities that exist are appointed by God" (Rom. 13:1). Let's teach it and believe it!

The Point—God is God-above-all and has the last word in all matters—whether a Republican or a Democrat is in the White House or controlling the Legislature.

2. Be thankful because God's Word calls us to be.

First Thessalonians 5:18 still commands, "In everything give thanks; for this is the will of God in Christ Jesus for you." Further, 1 Timothy 2:1-2 issues this clearest of all priorities upon believers: "I exhort first of all that [with prayers and intercession] giving of thanks be made…for kings and all who are in authority." There's no escaping the assignment—intercede, and do it *thankfully!*

The biblical call to intercession has never included the promise that we would be put in control of the answers— only that we could be assured of God's entry into the situation. Intercessory prayer is *not* to secure *our* will. Rather, intercession wars against the rule of blindness due to human sin and limitation. It resists the efforts of hell at mastering multitudes through dark powers and invites God's overruling. His sovereignty introduces redemptive possibilities, which we often do not see or understand until later.

The Point—Rejoice as you fast and pray, for in doing so, you partner with the Almighty in wise obedience to His Word. This action guarantees that the ultimate triumph of His ways will be unveiled in His time.

3. Be thankful.

Thank God for the possibilities that are unleashed when God's people take their proper stance in prayer, intercession and praise. (See 2 Chronicles 7:14; 1 Timothy 2:1-5.) Notwithstanding the edicts of human governments, a prayer-powered people will finally prevail. For example, a study of the Book of Daniel unveils the arrogance to which all human leaders and governments incline. But Nebuchadnezzer's pride and folly were later neutralized. The visitation of God's "overruling" that flowed into that ancient scene was due to believers (Daniel, Shadrach, Meshach and Abednego) who functioned *both* as active

participants in their earthly government and as transcendent citizens of the heavenly kingdom—unswerving in
their character, prayer and commitment to God's ways.

The Point—Irrespective of your delight or dismay or
whether you like a party's politics, you need to pray for
your government's leaders. God has called us not only to
thank Him for our leaders, but also to protect them from
human pride through our intercession for them.

Of course, nothing in these three points denies you or me
the privilege of differing with the actions or attitudes man-
ifested by those who govern us. The Bible is filled with
cases of people who submitted to political rule, but who
confronted or refused to bow before anything corrupting or
violating God's law. Furthermore, in our free land we have
the opportunity to participate in the political process in
order to see change effected as we may wish or pray for it
to be. Yet, the fact remains that God *never allows* us the privilege of bad-mouthing government, and He *does require us* to
pray and be thankful.

Besides, who of us can know or judge against the possibility
that Bill Clinton might be God's answer to our nation's present needs—regardless of your, my or his policies? Under

God's hand, and supported in prayer by *God's people,* he has a preferred chance at becoming *God's man* for the task.

Let's tend to our real business, leading our people to respond in obedience to God's eternal Word and not to surrender to political partisanship or emotional responses. Our nation is entering a new season, and it's no time for fainting, carping or gloating. In fact, it's the same time on the clock it's always been: *prayer time* and *praise time.*

Jack Hayford, "Praying for Our Leaders," *Ministries Today* (January/February 1993): 20–21.

[chapter 11] Our World and a "Watershed Moment"

I have the feeling we are coming to a watershed point in North American Christianity—one that will determine our ability to be heard as we seek to declare the redeeming word of the gospel. I believe the forward flow of the stream of the Spirit will either be released by a new discernment of our mission, or dammed and stagnated by a failure to remove a potential enculturated blockage.

In my preceding column, I noted the bewildering response of a host of devoted believers who were stunned, shaken, hopeless or angry over the results of the American presidential election. Many good people were too wrapped up in their political predispositions to see that God is still unshakably in charge of history, sovereign above all humanity's transient affairs. I wrote seeking to disentangle the temporal from the eternal.

Such political predispositions are not the only thing, however, that can deter pure vision and impede our mission. Our moral posturings can do the same.

Before I pursue this further, I need to assure you that...

1. **I am not arguing for a lower standard of righteous living among those of us who know and serve the Lord Christ.**

2. **I do not oppose the efforts of Christian ministries who feel called to oppose the forces undermining our culture's historic moral/ethical base.**

The watchdog efforts *and* evangelistic zeal of ministries to feel so called are greatly respected and often supported by my words and my wallet. But I am concerned about what "the world" is hearing from your lips and mine—from our sometimes stylized decryings of its state of affairs. Are they hearing us harp on their moral lassitude, or are they hearing the heavenly harp's chords of the angel's message: "I bring you good tidings of God's glory, peace and good will—the Savior's here"?

A Moral Mess

I'm pastoring in a town that has been a moral quagmire for so long that bombast and complaints about our nation's loss of "traditional values" or rejection of the "historic roots of American life" are virtually meaningless to the hearer. Such preachments as these, or any shows of indignation at either the liberal media or the homosexual lobby, don't fall on antagonistic ears as much as on *indifferent ones.* Such rumblings strike a great many people in our present culture as either arguments for our irrelevancy or testimonies to our intolerance.

This "cultural indifference" is not localized to metropolitan centers. The force and flow of the socializing dynamics around us have created the same basic moral venue for today's pastors, whether they serve in Dubuque or Detroit, Springfield or Seattle, Newcastle or New York.

The homogenization of public education and the public media have installed us amid a moral mess of pottage that our world has chosen for its diet. The question I want to discern is this: Am I called to rub the world's face in its stew, or am I commissioned to reach out with the health-giving bread and sweet wine of the gospel?

I really can't do both at once. I'm not likely to find any takers of God's holy, redeeming feast if their most recent memory is my reaching to splash the swill of their sin in their face. (And this is especially true since the world sees its "pottage" as gourmet dining!)

Something inside me is cautioning me these days—a heartbeat that seems to be pulsating with the compassion of Jesus rather than murmuring of moral cowardice. I've never been much of a political crusader anyway, but I'm becoming even more reticent to tout a moral platform other than one that features Good News—alone! And by "Good News" I mean the *essential* gospel of Jesus Christ—that God loves, that Jesus died to prove it, that He's alive to deliver all its satisfying goodness and soul-freeing power into the hands of all comers and that He is building a new, joyous community of those whose new birth ushers them into this vital, all-embracing family.

The Jesus Paradigm

I'm being reminded these days, as I've begun leading my flock through the Gospel of Matthew, that Jesus' business was not to *protest* but to *proclaim.* In fact, at the risk of seeming irreverent or undiscerning, I'm wondering which model for ministry the New Testament proposes—Jesus' or John's? Did John the Baptist miss recognizing a "watershed moment" in his time?

I've always thought of John as the epitome of fearless, forthright, "call-'sin'-sin" boldness. But his call to repentance was only understood in an environment where seeking souls were coming to hear—beside Bethabra's waters. When people are hungry for what you offer because they are sick of their diet of death, the call to turn from sin to God is understandable. But if the setting is changed, the same style can result in your being silenced. A paganized king, casually interested in a prophet's novelty but morally controlled by the convenience of his culture, is another arena—separate from the Bethabra bailiwick.

How do I heed the commission to become a "[child] of God without fault in the midst of a crooked and perverse nation" (Phil. 2:15), and at the same time "as much as depends on you, live peaceably with all men" (Rom. 12:18)? How did Jesus go about this business of eating with publicans and sinners, gaining a hearing in a hostile environment, yet keeping His values intact and His message unpolluted?

Of course, He was eventually silenced, too—temporarily. So the quest for the "Jesus paradigm" for ministry is not a quest for an easier course. The fact is that following the gospel call in a sinful world can cost any of us our lives. But Jesus wasn't killed by the systems of a pagan culture—He was crucified as a direct result of a prejudiced, religious one. And it is exactly that—the power of prejudiced religion to silence the compelling call of the Savior—that prompts my words here.

We may well be at the watershed point in our culture that John the Baptist missed seeing in his. As Jesus in no way demeaned John, He still made clear that His kingdom transcended the best John's message had to give. Perhaps our paganized world is not so much resistant to our call for "values," "historic traditions" and "the Judeo-Christian ethic" as it is incapable of understanding the desirability of those things.

But one thing almost every sinner understands and finds appealing is Jesus in the beauty of His person, in the tenderness of His compassion, in the power of His healing and delivering words.

Salt and Light

At the core of the issue is not a cheap or cowardly quest for survival, but a call to keep our heads clear—and on! I want us to maximize our ability to deliver our essential message for as long as our surrounding culture will hear us, by our actions testifying to and demonstrating our real, living, loving Lord. I propose that we will have infinitely more success at drawing souls to Him if we *show* His light with love and good works—rather than *shine* it in the world's face with the complaint that we wish they'd stop squinting their eyes, slapping us or turning their backs.

Nothing has changed as to the source of salt and light. It's still found solely in the people who have received the gospel of the kingdom. But salt, force-fed rather than sprinkled, is embittering; and light, glared rather than glowed, is blinding. So I've come to the conclusion that we are called to live our moral values before a world that isn't interested in receiving them (and even less so if they seem forced on them). In the meantime, while we're living morally, let's also give lovingly, giving every manner of good works to show the world we care about its hurt, its hunger, its homeless, its dying-from-AIDS hopelessness and even its blinded pursuit of hellishness.

Relevancy in ministry will be found by those who discern the difference between when we are *to light* and when we are *to fight.* If we fight the world in the public arena, rather than the powers of darkness in the prayer arena, we'll alienate our audience and end up with an empty house—however clean (Eph. 6:12). But if we light the world by love and good works, then multitudes who are now in the dark will tire of its evil and emptiness and look for a place to come in. Let's keep the light on for them.

Jack Hayford, "Which Harp Is Being Heard?" *Ministries Today* (March/April 1993): 24–25.

The Leader's Edge

The one danger a prayer leader needs to avoid is permitting an elitist or mystical spirit to find place among those banded for prayer. The spiritual dynamism, depth of insight and intense passion *power-praying* brings is, indeed, *vital,* but it can turn *vicious* if untempered by a human realism. Being realistic about our "mere humanity" means remembering our clay feet, our capacity for deluding self-importance and religious pomposity. That's why I've included the next two articles—each focuses our finiteness and will likely cheer all who are honest enough to confess their human limitations. Though grand realms of God-allowed privilege are granted through prayer's partnership with His almightiness, we all encounter things less than conducive to constant success in keeping focus in prayer. So, as I've noted, as surely as the human tongue can call for "great and mighty things" (Jer. 33:3), it is wise to occasionally put it in our cheek, and there remember what God never forgets about us: We're still "dust" (Ps. 103:14).

For More...

To help keep a daily focus in prayer, a team of friends helped me formulate *Celebrate! Daily Devotions for the Spirit-Filled Life,* a 365-day devotional guide published by Thomas Nelson.

[chapter 12]

Ever Have "Wand'ring Tho'ts"?

LET me be humblingly frank: I suffer with "wandering thoughts." Do you? Let me be clear before you answer, because I'm not referring to carnal wrestlings with impurity. That's a struggle we've all faced, and hopefully overcome, but that's not the point here. Neither am I talking about being bored by a wearying lecturer or a dry sermon. Rather, I'm talking about having my mind wander when I'm in the presence of the Almighty.

Most frustrating is when it happens early—when I'm up in the morning and attempting to earnestly, sincerely, devotedly and faithfully pray. Do you know what I mean? I'm talking about the too-many-times-to-count episodes of starting to pray—and then...then..."Let's see, where was I?"

Wandering thoughts in the presence of God can be incredibly guilt-inducing. I suppose some would say, "And rightly so! How insulting to His Holiness!"

But I don't believe that. And the reason I don't is because of something that happened a while back.

It was one of those days—a morning of wandering thoughts. After beginning to feel condemned for my human vulnerability to a lost focus, I stopped in the middle of my muddle and decided I wouldn't offend Him any more than I may have already done if I took the matter straight to the Lord Himself. "Lord, I feel so...so *dumb*...so insensitive and unspiritual when this happens." And, bless His gentle graciousness, He helped me—but He also did something more. He whispered comfort and assurance to my soul, a comfort and assurance I later sought to capture in the simplicity of the following poetic piece.

Since then, its circulation has brought encouragement to many who have attested that the poem brought a new assurance of God's patience with their frailties and a new confidence that such days are not insulting to Him or violative of our appropriate humility before Him. So, I'm relaying it here. It's not intended as an excuse for mental sloth, but as a comfort to us who, on some occasions, find it inexplicably hard to "gird up" our minds when we're trying to start the day right with Jesus.

Wand'ring Tho'ts

I bring my scattered tho'ts today, O Lord, let them be
   prayers.

It seems I can't do better, for my mind runs everywhere.

I've started at Your Throne five times, I guess, and then
   I've wandered

from pole to pole. My mind has strolled and half an
   hour squandered.

I feel I've wasted time when I begin then don't go
   heav'ward.

And now I sit here puzzled. (Can You see me? Are You
   here, Lord?)

I've wondered if it counts, if You, dear Father, know
   I'm trying;

If wand'ring tho'ts are ever "prayer"—or just "dis-
   qualifying."

I fear at times I'm too much flesh, and far too weak in
   spirit,

unless somehow my wand'ring mind translates to
   prayer—(Lord, hear it?)

It flits from pointed praying to some thoughts about a
   friend

I'll see today. (His problem hurts my heart—When will
   it end?)

That thought becomes a springboard to a time ten years
   ago

when someone else I know was here (When was it—
    spring or fall?).

Ah, fall...but, now it's summertime. Just listen to
    those birds.

This lovely morn their singing prompts my pen—I
    write these words:

Remember to buy dog food for the pup this after-
    noon.

And while downtown, pick up the package—Oh, dear
    Lord, I've zoomed!

From this decade to that, and from one season to
    another,

I ended with a dog, when starting prayer for one dear
    brother.

What do You think, Lord, of this child, whose mind's so
    awfully flabby?

(Of course, it's not always this way, You know, Lord—all
    this shabby.)

I have some days when worship soars and intercession
    presses

to take the kingdom e'en by force—as faith-filled prayer
    possesses;

Possesses promised land You've said will surely yield to
    them

whose warfare strikes hell's battlelines, and boldly
    enters in—

In to seize sure vict'ry's prize, the rescue of men's
    souls;

and through travailing prayer attain a dozen other
   goals.

Yes, I've had times of power-prayer. But God, what of
   this season?

—This morning when my wand'ring tho'ts seem void of
   rhyme or reason.

I sit here in this armchair, and while looking on the
   lawn,

the sunlight sends a crystal beam...the dew makes
   rainbows...God!

God, look! I'm off again! O Lord, forgive my wand'ring
   so.

"Gird up!" I shout. "Now, every thought, I take you
   captive—NOW!

Become obedient unto Christ!" I harsh-command my
   brain.

"Stop wand'ring!" (What was that? The cat? I must let
   Fluffy in.)

Good morning, kitty. Need some milk? (Oh, look the
   paper's there

beside the porch. I'll get it, quick, though in my under-
   wear!)

The cat is fed. The dog's outside. Now back to
   prayer...what's that?

The headline of the paper says the President is back.

But lay that paper down now, soul; you're not done
   with your praying.

Back to my knees. I'm here now, Lord...Let's see—what
    was I saying?

Oh, yes. I'm here to ask You, Lord, if wand'ring tho'ts
    count with You?

Could You just let me know You care I got up to be
    near You?

I came because I love You, Lord; my poor mind
    notwithstanding.

My heart is Yours, so please, these tours of mine—be
    understanding.

And somehow in the silence—(There's the neighbor's
    car now, leaving.)

I think...indeed, I do; I hear a Voice—Lord, I'm
    receiving!

I do receive Your comfort: "Lo, I'm always with you,
    child."

I do receive Your peace, Lord: "Rest, altho' your mind
    runs wild.

For I am still your God, and still My eye scans earth for
    hearts,

not minds. For human intellect, at best, is so
    'in part.'

I loathe no mind, but neither honor thoughts that have
    no love;

and no mind pierces heaven—only hearts ascend
    above.

So, don't despair, child—Yes! This hour just passed does
    count with Me.

I also care about your pup, and for your hungry
　　kitty.

"Those actions may not be a prayer, but neither are
　　they sinning.
And I deem worthy service unto Me your day's begin-
　　nings.
I heard your heart pray for your friend. And when you
　　saw the dew,
I liked that; as through wand'ring tho'ts I've strolled
　　along with you.
I don't mind simply being here: all lovers have their
　　memories
of simply sitting silently to share each other's
　　reveries.
You'll gird for war another day; you'll move in bold
　　advance
against dark pow'rs. (Remember, when you do, they
　　have no chance!)

"But on this day of wand'ring tho'ts, be pleased to rest
　　in Me;
for I'm the God of all of you, since you love all
　　of Me."[7]

Jack Hayford, "Ever Had Wandering Thoughts?" *Ministries Today*,
July/August 1996): 19.

[chapter 13]

Silence and Sensibility

NO, that title above isn't the name of a Jane Austen novel. But it does prompt a discussion that deals with sense and sensibility and, rightly applied, is sure to humble pride and smash prejudice! But enough punning, however true the jibes. Straight on, now: How do you listen for the voice of God? How do you gain a sense of His direction, with an assurance you are being *sensible* and not merely *sensual?*

I'm not appealing for a mystic's answer, and I don't need a rebuke from a literalist impugning my suggestion that God speaks in any other way than through the Bible. Of course you and I know and affirm that God's written Word is the final authority on how we interpret or apply any prompting we may receive by His "voice." The Scriptures are the grid by which all words, visions, dreams or other guidance are to be measured for truth or counsel.

But that point of wisdom doesn't discount the fact, nor

should it ever discourage our expectancy, that God does "speak" to people today.

I don't think I've ever met an effective spiritual leader whose plans and pursuits aren't influenced by "leadings"— that is, to use my terminology, "the voice of the Lord." While His ways and means of dealing with us differ, and how we may each describe His "speaking" is widely varied, I believe most of us depend on "a word from God" with regularity.

How do you receive or "hear" His voice to you?

(Excuse me a moment, the phone just rang.)

(OK, I'm back now.)

My personal focus on the subject is born of a deep desire you probably share with me: I want to be "on target"—tuned to God's heart and purpose—in my life. Still, I've just gone through a recent season of struggling in my own soul as I have waited on God for His direction. The candid truth is that it often takes me months to gain peace on a matter—to find a restful confidence that I have the Lord's mind on major issues I face, personally and pastorally.

(Oops—phone again, and just as the garbage truck is grinding its compactor in front of my house, too.)

Further, while engaged personally in my own pursuit of God's will, I've wondered a good bit about impressions I receive from the Bible—and from some leaders I've listened to. I mean, does it ever seem to you that everyone *but* you has access to a hotline to heaven? ("And God said, 'Abraham, Abraham,' and Abraham answered and said…" [See Genesis 22:1-2.])

Gaining Certainty

I certainly don't begrudge anyone the blessing of instant, perfect direction if and when they get it. But as often as I do receive spontaneous insight, wisdom and promptings during church services or messages (and witness the Holy Spirit's confirmation), I don't find that major issues in my personal life are usually addressed very quickly. Gaining certainty that I've "heard right" takes me time to process— sometimes weeks of simply leaving a matter before God's throne, while recurrently coming back there to wait, silently, until His peace gradually settles a matter in my heart and mind.

But silence is hard to come by.

Just this morning, having risen early, I stepped outside in the relative stillness of the dawn—hoping for an "in the garden" experience (you know, "and He walks with me and He talks with me"). But the distant, dull groan of the freeway traffic a mile away crept in and around my neighborhood, distracting me from the peacefulness of my otherwise quiet yard.

Be Still and Know

Oh, I know God isn't restricted to idyllic settings when communicating His will and way to us. I'm not looking for a *mood* in order to receive a *message.* But I am concerned for all of us who lead today—concerned that we not lose the sensitivity to our Sovereign that only comes in times of silence before Him.

"Be still, and know that I am God" (Ps. 46:10). "In quietness and confidence shall be your strength" (Isa. 30:15). "Wait, I say, on the Lord!" (Ps. 27:14). These are still in the Book— and like so much of our life in Christ, the rewards of promise only proceed from the disciplines of obedience.

Yet "being still" doesn't come easily. In fact, the actions, words and styles of some leaders I've observed seem to suggest they'd consider this order of stillness passé—or unnecessary for those who are "really tuned in."

I began to list things I see that seem to hinder our spiritual sensitivity as leaders. Amid the plethora of information downloading over our heads and the numbing-to-the-soul "noise" of everything from events shouting for our attention to jets thundering overhead (one just did, here), a prophet's ear for the voice of the Lord is hard to cultivate.

(Excuse me, the doorbell.)

(I'm back. It was the UPS man with new speakers for the stereo.)

I want to emphasize that these words aren't a whimper of complaint. They are a call born of my own recent soul-searching, a statement, of sorts, declaring my intent not to be caught in the vortex of converging sounds or the furious whirlwind of activities, however righteous. The shaping of everything from this Sunday's sermon to the balance of my life requires waiting—waiting in the Presence, stilled and seeking, listening for the whispers.

So if any of this encourages you—either hearing how my noisy world sounds much like yours or noting that my concern resonates with your own spirit's quest for seeking Him, in silence, in the secret place of His holy pavilion—then I'm grateful.

At the very least, may your heart be assured that "to wait on God" at times, hesitantly and cautiously, is not a surrender to a wimpish walk with the Almighty. It's often a noisy one with clattering or disrupting distractions, but the "waiting and listening" soul will always be rewarded. His voice is still louder than the tempest.

That's it. I'll be quiet.

Peace.

Jack Hayford, "Silence and Sensibility," *Ministries Today* (September/October 1996): 20–21.

The Leading Edge

Because of God-graced privilege, some church leaders like myself appear to be living in the midst of "the big" (such as pastoring a church of thousands, speaking to stadium crowds in the tens of thousands and ministering via the media to millions). To the outside viewer, it is possible that sight be lost of the fact that no wise leader, however privileged, ever perceives "the crowd" as either a definition of his or her ministry or identity. Leaders who outlast those who became "famous" are those who have found constancy in the private place of an integrous walk with God. Just as I have shared this value with leaders around the world, I offer this pair of excerpts from my journal—explaining something of the context of each, but mostly simply explaining something of the highest values of my heart.

For More...

No more electric time ever occurred in my decades of pastoral teaching than during the three Sundays I sat on a high stool, distributed outlined material to the congregation and shared practical guidance for cultivating a daily quiet time with the Lord. *Our Daily Walk* is a small book providing that resource.[8] It is available in audio form as "The Renewal of Devotional Habit."

[chapter 14]

Journaling a Private Revival

"THE spirit of faith is being released, and the sweetness of Holy Ghost renewal and restoration is beginning to be tasted!"

I wrote those words one morning as they naturally rose in my soul. They were part of a time of distinct renewing—a "private revival," you might say, and I want to share something of that season. It was a period of several weeks—a season of the Holy Spirit's dealing with, shaping, shaking and stirring me, and this is my personal testimony.

While being moved upon during those weeks, I one day found, while journaling, a difficulty in coming by "words"— that is, words sufficient to describe what was taking place. The fresh surgings in my soul weren't the result of a visit to any of the places or meetings that many people have recently sought to find spiritual refreshing. In fact, I hadn't been anywhere but home. It began on the Saturday night of our annual Conference on Spirit-Filled Living at The Church On The Way. That night something unusual happened to me.

A Visitation of "Newness"

In the preceding weeks, a gnawing hunger and a haunting sense of expectancy had been stirring around the edges of my soul. Then came June 13. I was standing in the front row of the congregation as prayer was being offered at the service's conclusion. Suddenly, simply, softly and quietly, something I can only describe as *newness* swept over and throughout my entire inner man. It was difficult to describe—a distinct "feeling"—yet more than merely a sensation. It was something internal, transcendent and real. At the same time, in the stillness of that moment, a prophetic word was whispered to my inner man: "Tell everyone, *today* is the beginning of 'the *new* The Church On The Way.'" There was *nothing* of "gimmick" in the phrase, and I *did* relate it to the gathered throng—making clear it was not a "word" calling so much for immediate action as for a readiness to receive the future with an availability to change, flexibility and expectancy.

But more significant to me was what I felt happening to me, in me and through me. I didn't try to explain what I had felt, but I knew it *was* very much of God—very much a *call* to open to and seek Him! The "feeling" I described was more than

THE PENETRATING EDGE—THE LEADER'S PATHWAY TO POWER

momentary. It continued intermittently within me for about three days. I hesitate to mention that, because I do not believe transient manifestations are to be sought, depended upon or repeated. It's the kind of misguidedness that turns many revival manifestations into "dependencies" of the immature and makes idols of those who advocate or experience them. However, as a "sign" to me (and I *do* believe in *signs*), it did evidence something more than merely a moment's impression.

Beyond that, however, the greatest significance was what began to develop over the coming six weeks—there was a marked, deep working of His Spirit taking place within me. [And while editing even now, over three years later, the confirmations of the "new" at The Church On The Way have been abundant, mighty and marvelously fruitful…and He is *still* calling us as a body, beckoning unto tomorrows of high promise.]

Most moving to me at the time, however, was that I felt He was speaking to me, not simply by reason of my leader role, but (I couldn't help but feel) probably because, in His eyes, I was the one most needy of "newness"! During the ensuing weeks, as the Holy Spirit began to process this impacting moment of spiritual quickening, things transpired that not only impacted me personally, but also distilled transferable teaching I want to offer you. Let me share this teaching the way it was fixed in my understanding as I journaled my thoughts at the time.

I am discovering the joy of being *"pruned"* as a branch, *"refined"* as silver, *"burned"* as chaff, *"circumcised"* as a child and *"flooded"* as a riverbed. Each of these phrases, whispered to my heart during recent times of devotion, has proved to be laden with meaning to my soul. It's tempting to preach them too soon, but for the appropriate time, I will record the concepts here, noting the scriptural meaning and personal significance of each.

Pruning is that action of the Father by which the means of former fruit-bearing is cut away in order to make way for a new season of fruitfulness (John 15:1-2). In this the Spirit confronts our tendency to protect past systems or methodologies in order to unveil the Creator's new ways and workings.

God's *refining process* removes "dross"—the frothy residue of imbedded material that reduces the purity and value of truly worthy silver (Mal. 3:3). There are beauties of God's created purpose in each of us, submerged by the compacted dust of our human nature. These are only released to mirror magnificently the Savior's image when the fire of the Spirit's deeper working drives out the unworthy.

Chaff is the external husk that may protect the head of wheat during its growth season, but which must be crushed and removed in order to garner the fruit of the harvest (Luke 3:17). Chaff must burn away for God to visit me. Just as in Jesus' day, the same requirement precedes any real visitation of God today. I ask, "Lord, what of the external in my own life and practice needs crushing in order to give place to the entry of Your kingdom with power?"

Circumcision is the Old Testament covenant expression adapted in the New Testament to the heart (Col. 2:11). It is God's way of saying that surplus flesh, extraneous and unnecessary to His reproductive processes through my life, must be surgically removed. It requires no remarkable insight to grasp the message here—only honesty. The flesh must be categorically and conclusively dealt with in order for His New Covenant life and blessing to be released.

The *flooding* of the riverbed of the soul springs from the fountainhead of the Spirit's overflowings, about which Jesus prophesied (John 7:37-39). As I have opened up to the newness of my current experience of refreshing, I was amazed to discover how earlier habits of "praying in the Spirit" (Jude 20; 1 Cor. 14:15) and "singing with the Spirit" (Eph. 5:19; 1 Cor. 14:15) had been neglected. I was stirred to assertively give place to the rivers of refreshing, welling up from the inner man, penetrating and overflowing my whole personality in times of private prayer.

With this cluster of private probings came an ongoing, week-to-week series of reminders—of being called afresh to known basics. These basics had suffered unperceived neglect to the point that "first love" vitality was lacking.

Among them, thanks to the Holy Spirit's quickening, two more significant "refresher courses" are being personally applied.

1. *Drinking more deeply from the Word.* I am now drinking deeper and deeper draughts of the water of the Word. I am remembering, "The flood tide of Holy Spirit workings flows out of the river of revelation in the Scriptures." I always read the Word daily, but I have been reading far more and being rewarded wonderfully. It is such a joy to experience the reality of tides of the Spirit surging through me as I read more and more of the Word He has breathed!

2. *Pursuing God more earnestly.* Further, I have been reminded all over again that pursuing God is a prerequisite to finding Him. These texts have loomed large to my mind as I have heard His voice:

You will seek Me and find Me, *when you search for Me with all your heart.*

—JEREMIAH 29:13, EMPHASIS ADDED

As the deer pants for the water brooks, so pants my soul for You, O God.

—PSALM 42:1, EMPHASIS ADDED

I [must] press toward the goal.

—PHILIPPIANS 3:14

There is a common denominator to these Bible verses— they make clear that *asking, seeking* and *knocking* are *not casual exercises.* As a result, I have been rising earlier and with more excitement and expectation, knowing He is calling me to something more of Himself and something "new" in His purposes for me and those I lead.

All in all, I feel I am only beginning to test new dimensions of the wealth—the riches of His presence and purpose. The things the Lord has dealt with me about have a common denominator: They are each born of the essence of that passion that "hungers and thirsts for righteousness." Responded to, they carry the certainty of "fullness"—of discovering "the kingdom" entering with power into their private world. Once again, I stand renewed and reminded of the timeless fact: I will only be filled with as much of God as I want.

One more thing: this journaling needs a context, because in relaying it I offer it as *both* an encouragement and a summons to any leader who needs "newness" as I did. So, let me explain. I wasn't backslidden. That's not a self-righteous defense, but simply to say I don't even think the Lord Himself would have said I was chilled in my soul or without a warm devotion to Him. Nonetheless, He said I needed *"newness,"* and in His grace He called me to a new season of my soul—a grace that assisted my response and brought remarkable refreshing. He awakened me to a renewed and deeper desire to seek Him. Even more, He renewed my understanding of how fulfilling and enriching personal renewal can be as we rediscover how inexhaustible a source of refreshing and fulfillment our Lord Jesus is.

So I leave my testimony with you. It's the story of an encounter, and of a series of weeks as I responded to it. I found a feast of *newness,* and my deep conviction is that there's something of the same there for any who come— "feelings" or no. Because when it comes to *newness,* with Jesus, "new" is never mere novelty—it's His "best." As the Creator of the feast, He always saves the best for last—His most recent vintage of the wine of His Spirit being made fully available for each of us who will seek Him anew.

Jack Hayford, "Journaling a Private Revival," *Ministries Today* (September/October 1998): 22–23.

[chapter 15]   All My Earthbound Senses

GOD has created us as *sensory beings*—creatures who interact with the world through the physical senses of sight, sound, taste, smell and touch. But that doesn't mean we're to become *sensual persons*. There's a world of difference between being *sensory* and being *sensual*. The first is tuned to God's creation; the second is tarnished by the world's corruption.

At the end of this year's spring season, I passed another milestone in life—my birthday is in late June. It seems I've been automatically provided with two excellent prompters—New Year's Day and my birthday, about one-half year apart. These occasions prompt me to take seriously the wisdom of David's words: "Search me, O God, and know my heart; try me, and know my anxieties; and see if there is any wicked way in me, and lead me in the way everlasting" (Ps. 139:23-24). At such times I seek to give the Holy Spirit time to do a "soul search" on my system—a counterpart to what my doctor does in my semiannual physical exam.

At my most recent "inner-man checkup," I became very aware of how numbed my spiritual sensitivities can become through the exposure of my physical senses to the world around me. In pressing me toward a new level of sensitivity to Him, the Holy Spirit brought to mind an occasion ten years ago.

I had just embarked on my return flight from Cairo, Egypt, having been there to minister to several hundred Arab pastors. Somewhere above the Mediterranean, heading north on a course over Greece and into Frankfurt, Germany, my heart began to swell with a gratitude to God for my five physical senses. As I meditated on the capacities our Creator has willed us as *sensory* beings, I was moved to praise, writing my heartfelt joy in a poem I titled "All My Earthbound Senses, Lord."

A Thickened Soul

In contrast to this episode, however, a more recent heart search brought me face to face with the tormenting capacity that those same senses have to make me a *sensual* person. I hasten to add—though not defensively or for shame, but simply for clarity's sake—that by coming to terms with inclinations to "sensuality," I don't mean to imply a struggle with sexually expressed sensuality. Of course, I'm not suggesting that I need to discipline this vulnerability any less in my own life than I suppose you may need to do so in yours. But still, the issue was greater than this one arena—it was the broad spectrum to which our senses gravitate for satiation rather than finding their use and expression in the originally intended, created order of things.

I was stirred to the core of my awareness at how "thickened" my soul can become—how callused against sensitivity to the Holy Spirit. I realized this "thickness" is caused by the indulgence of my physical senses: what I allow myself to hear, to see, to feel, to taste or to smell.

I was reminded of a particular conversation—one I could have aborted at the point that words became inappropriate. But I enjoyed *listening* to the words that, while not evil, still fed something less than worthy in my inner being. Then my heart was pricked by another recollection: a quick pass-by of a TV channel at which I stopped for less than five seconds. But I did stop, allowing my eyes the input of something so "other than" what my life is about that I felt embarrassed—even though I was alone.

Spiritual Checkup

These insights about the way my natural senses can dull my spiritual sensitivity prompted an extensive prayer, which I inscribed in my journal. While it wasn't written for publication purposes (and not all of it is here) I want to relate it in part. Perhaps as a fellow servant of the King, and as a leader who longs to sustain a high level of spiritual sensitivity to God's Word and ways, you might draw from this prayer somehow. I wrote:

> **Dear Lord God, at this portal of new possibility and promise...**
>
> *My eyes feel "scaled" and needful of surgery.*
>
> **Jesus, You whose eyes burn with heaven's fire, look into mine and burn off the overlay of film that has accumulated. Forgive me for abusing this sensory capacity by ever looking on anything Your holy eyes would never tolerate. Forgive me for "scanning" superficially when human need is present before me; for watching a documentary on hunger and death, for example, and becoming capable of "seeing" agony, but through repeated exposure to it becoming progressively less sensitized to its awfulness. Lord, give me "eyes to see," lest I succumb to the emptiness of soul of those who "having eyes, they see not—and having ears, they hear not."**
>
> *With my ears, Lord, I want to hear more clearly than ever.*
>
> **Flush from my soul's hearing channels the wax that can clutter and clog; the accumulated loss of "directness" that misses the whispers of the Holy Spirit's promptings—the sounds of Your wisdom that You speak in the silence. I live in the rush and din of a hurried, harried, verbose, pomp-and-palaver-filled world, Lord. Soften the hardened, scarred tissue rendered insensitive by the**

occupational hazard of serving in a realm of "too much talk" and "too little listen." Let me hear heaven's songs when I'm with You, and let me sound the depths of Your heart as my soul's ears hear Your Word as it speaks to me from the open pages of Your Book.

I feel my hands are gloved, Lord.

I know that You are seeking hands through which to touch, but my desire for Your power to course through mine seems unanswered at times. Could it be, Jesus, that You seek cleaner or more tender hands through which to work? I feel it's so and come with mine uplifted, Lord. As I present my hands in Your presence, wash every crease, and reprogram my touch. Forgive my soul's "manhandling" of things holy, and imprint my fingertips with Yours, transforming my identity to reveal that You are there when I reach to another in Your name.

My tastes are jaded, I fear.

"Though I speak with the tongues of men and angels," another "tongue"—my soul's taste preferences and lip-smacking lust for approval by others—seems to slobber its crudity around my life. But, Lord, You're the one who "loosed" the tongues of men bound physically from speech, so to You I come for release from any soul bonds—either to "tastes" that would prohibit my availability to any place You want me to serve, or to "tastes" that would inhibit my readiness toward any person you want me to love.

My soul has a "nose," too.

Just as surely as a seasonal cold can clog my sinuses and remove my sense of smell, so, Lord, I fear that coldness of heart has at times dulled my soul's "nasal discernment." Sin that ought to smell like sewage to me can for a moment seem almost alluring, while the fragrance of Your presence—so worth seeking in extended times of waiting on You—too easily becomes a passively appreciated joy.

Lord, heal my whole soul—that every sense be alive to You and every sensitivity be alert to Your will.

Spring Cleaning

Springtime is an usually sense-oriented season—the warmth of the ascending sun being felt anew following the winter's cold; the flowering splendor all around us inviting our sight, smell and touch; the sweetness of the air seeming almost to satisfy our tongue's taste buds! So with this season, I invite you to take an inventory of the blessings of our sensory capacities—but especially to weigh those capabilities as they find expression in the soul.

Jack Hayford, "All My Earthbound Senses," *Ministries Today* (May/June 1993): 8–9.

Section 3
Cutting to the Core

*Facing Leadership Issues
and Demands*

Just as leaders need to *grow* and leaders need to *pray,* leaders need to *think.* Thinking *clearly* and *thinking through* are a tandemed team. If either is omitted, the mind's function becomes as a cart with a broken wheel—progress screeches to a halt, the load spills, and you stand there with whatever is lost, smashed or ruined. Clear thinking starts with God's Word. Thorough thinking requires a commitment to God's ways. The counsel of others, of history or tradition, and the counsel of the heart willing to remain correctable by God's Spirit—these converge to carve deeply into life and thought, and to resolve core issues rightly.

A wide spectrum of subjects are set forth in these eight articles, but they have a common denominator to my view. Without coming to terms with issues *like* these—and certainly, with *all* these—a leader will fall into a murky mind-set and end up being governed by the slothful or sensual decision making.

The Leader's Edge

Let's start by *thinking clearly* about our role amid a crisis. Leaders in *every* profession are being misguided and often shipwrecked by our culture's casual attitude toward marital commitment. This article was written in the wake of my hearing of *six* leaders departing their marriages—*in one week!* It is *not* a preachment, but a compassionate *appeal*. An injection of God's healing power can reverse things and restore wholeness—by acknowledging the marital priorities in God's Word.

For More...

Gary Smalley's marriage weekends for couples and his remarkable videotape series have helped multitudes find health and build strength in their marriage.[9] Pastoral leaders might investigate a week at SonScape Re-Creation Ministries, a ministry to pastoral pairs *before* problems overtake them.[10]

At *The King's Seminary*, Anna and I conduct a three-and-one-half-day *Consultation*—transparently sharing life, our experiences and truth from God's Word as we seek to nurture strong pastor-couples.[11]

[chapter 16]

Crisis in Marital Fidelity

THE recent rash of marital failures among high-profile spiritual leaders is forcing a showdown in the church. It isn't a showdown between those who have failed and those who might criticize them—it's a confrontation needed to face down a murky mind-set clouding the horizon, which, if unchanged, will bring a hurricane of hellish delusion.

Exactly what is happening anyway—and why? Precisely what ought to and can be done about it—and how? And what consequences could distill if discerning, decisive action is not taken now—especially among believers in the "Spirit-filled" sector of the church?

The Present Crisis

In regard to attitudes about leaders and marriage, there is no way to describe the present moment in lesser terms: *We are at a point of crisis!* Names are neither necessary nor appropriate here, but the full spectrum has been spanned—from renowned evangelical Bible preachers to Charismatic evangelists, from noted national youth leaders to ascending Christian television superstars. Though the unprecedented *general* increase in the number of broken marriages or moral failures occurring among church leaders is tragic enough, the crisis is amplified when high-visibility leaders go in and out of marriages. Sheep follow shepherds, and multitudes mime the more visible. Thus, hereby innumerable struggling couples reduce their resolve to resist society's indifference to divorce or immorality as the collapse of their "spiritual heroes'" marriages seem to justify, if not normalize, those same practices. Comfortableness, convenience and human counsel replace commitment, constancy and the place of the cross in the marriage.

At the center of this crisis, confused and biblically unfocused thinking is amplifying the impact of the above sadnesses. It begins with understandable sympathies appropriately shown for fallen or broken leaders. Loving concern for the present and future of such leaders is fitting—a response with love, grace and generosity. But in too many quarters lacking the necessary balance or schooling in Bible-based disciplines, blinded or intentionally neglectful attitudes waive the application of the wisdom and truth needed to rightly serve the moment. The same attitudes dissipate what is essential to sustain the pure passion and dynamic vitality of the church. Several issues rise in the middle of this muddle:

- First is the widespread unawareness of the *priority* of clearly stated biblical qualifications for a person to move into leadership ministry. Companion to this is the lost emphasis on the intrinsic relationship between a spiritual leader's marital commitment and moral fidelity as fundamentally required for continued ministry.

- Second, many deny or refuse to apply these *leader-standards* when they have been violated. Whether the failure was due to marital stress or outright sin, feelings are allowed rule rather than biblical principles, and true life-restoring ministry is preempted. Wise and righteous dealings—graciously removing a leader from ministry (for healing, counsel or other supportive care) and then weighing the hope of an eventual restoration of the leader following the moral failure, separation or divorce—are disdained as either impractical or "too hard to apply," and humanistic means substituted for divine directives.

- Third, the issue of imminent consequences of even more drastic error appears to be already present. If sound, scriptural administration of the issues surrounding the church, its leaders and their marriages is not soon arrived at with solidarity, there is reason to prophesy widespread deception on other subjects as well. The "itching ears" forecast for the last days represents the "tickle me with ideas but don't call me to

character or maturity" mind-set of some on today's church landscape, and is a setup for delusion by error.

Place and Priority

The reported response of one leader recently divorced (only to remarry within one week!) seems to have been convincing enough to justify his actions in the eyes of his followers: "God didn't call me to marriage—He called me to ministry!" There are multiple ironies in such an unbiblical utterance given in such a compromised circumstance, but the bottom line reads out with a sad reality—several thousand people "bought it." These presumably did so on the grounds that they either thought the idea was a spiritual one or didn't care if it was or not.

In contrast to the glibness suggesting a nobility in "dedication to ministry over marriage," the truth of God's Word casts the issue in vastly different light. According to the Scriptures, if a leader is married, two things are foundational:

1. **The commitment he/she shows toward his/her marriage *determines that person's right to lead* as a servant of Christ *in* the church.**
2. **The quality he/she reveals of his/her will to grow in marriage *determines the manner that person will model* as a representative of Christ *to* the church.**

There is no escaping the two-edged truth unveiled in the New Testament. Since heaven's Bridegroom has come to earth to win a bride for Himself, the principles of commitment (faith) and constancy (growth) are "locked" in the imagery of the marriage covenant between a man and a woman. Further, no one is more accountable to learn and grow in the lifestyle of modeling this commitment than a leader given by Christ to serve His bride. No "gifts" of a brilliant leader, however remarkable, ought to be allowed to substitute for the will to increase in the graces required for two different humans to grow together. No "fruit" of statistical achievement is a worthy replacement for the required development of "the fruit of the Spirit" needed for a husband and wife to learn to live together for a lifetime.

Ephesians 5:20–33 not only points to the demanding nature of commitment needed by husband and wife to make a marriage work, but it also concludes with these sweeping words: "I speak concerning Christ and the church" (v. 32)! Forty years of experience and observation of leaders have taught me one profound fact in this regard: A married leader will eventually and inevitably treat Jesus' bride the way he treats his own. And one who is a parent will also teach and lead the family of God the same way she does her own children. (Switch genders in both statements—it is the same either way.)

Faith and Commitment

The Ephesians 5 idea of *true faith* in Christ, and His *faithful commitment* to His own, is inextricably linked throughout God's Word to the figure of a faithful, growing marriage. Jesus communicated this idea in His parable of the returning bridegroom. (See Matthew 25:1-13.) His use of the figure fills the bridegroom/bride relationship with more than passion—the central issue is *fidelity to a promise* on the groom's part and *constancy of devotion* on the bride's. The message: Time can dampen fervor, but true love transcends emotion and remains committed.

Again, the living faith is basically a marriage throughout the Bible, beginning with the type depicted in Eve's creation from Adam's side (foreshadowing Christ's begetting His bride through His wounded side). It sustains until the finale, for we all anticipate our first stop beyond this world's history at a grand dinner called "The Marriage Supper of the Lamb" (Rev. 19:9). The message there? Tribulations rise and fall, but joy will come in the morning—hang tough!

Another great Old Testament text focuses this image. In Jeremiah 3:14, God's commitment to the backslider is, "I'm married to you!"—a statement that calls a leader to seek to sustain his/her marriage, though society argues, "If it's not fun anymore, trash it!" It's a tender issue, and we are certainly never to condemn a divorced or fallen leader. But neither can we permit a casual treatment of their tragedy. God's Word is never to be lightly regarded on these points: How a believer *lives* unto Christ is measured in terms of marital fidelity, and how a leader *leads* in His name is to be judged by the same!

Expected of Leaders

Though often cavalierly dismissed by the careless or uninformed among Jesus' church, the Word gives requirements that serve as a grid for measuring a spiritual leader's readiness to lead. First Timothy 3:1–15 and Titus 1:5–16 list standards incumbent upon every leader who would serve in Christ's church. This is true regardless of what Ephesians 4:11 office they serve. The positional terms in Timothy and Titus—"bishop" (*episkopos,* overseer), "deacon" (*diakonos,* minister), "elder" (*presbuteros,* mature leader)—form a cluster of at least a dozen behavioral requirements that, at the very least, establish a *minimal* standard for any and all spiritual leaders. They span everything from being nonargumentative, noncombative and humbly teachable (as well as capable to teach) to being a faithful spouse and a good parent.

Equally important is the context: 1 Timothy 3:10 calls for *time* to verify these qualities; 1 Timothy 5:22 calls for *slowness* to confirm a person to leadership. Further, if through problem, stress, tragedy or personal failure a leader pointedly violates or is unable to fulfill the biblical standard, he/she is to be relieved of ministry—at least for an extended season. If for no other reason than to grant a needed period for spiritual and/or emotional healing, this policy ought to be regarded today. Reinstatement may eventually come, since the hope of recovery is so characteristic of God's gracious, redemptive ways, but not without an extended season of recovery.

An even more thoughtful look at these leadership qualifications leads to seeing they have more to say about marriage responsibilities than the immediately obvious. First, certain *direct* statements do declare absolute requirements: 1) faithfulness in marital commitment (1 Tim. 3:2, 12; Titus 1:6); and 2) orderly leadership in raising his/her children (1 Tim.

3:4-5, 12; Titus 1:6). Indirectly, but certainly no less significantly, *most of the whole list applies to marriage.* For example, being "hospitable" represents an attitude of prioritizing time with one's spouse and family as much as it does welcoming people into your home (1 Tim. 3:2; Titus 1:8). Being "gentle" (1 Tim. 3:3) and "not quick-tempered" (Titus 1:7) calls for a private "loving as Christ loved the church" spirit toward one's husband/wife (Eph. 5:25-29) just as much as for a public graciousness or self-control with members of the congregation.

Whether we like it or not, our spiritual leaders are expected to meet more of a standard than the world sets for its leading figures. If these requirements are not being met *in at least an initial and growing way,* the married leader's potential for placement is to be disallowed. Perfection or full maturity is not mandated, but neither is it enough that he/she be exempted from any of the standards because they "are so anointed!" (So was Balaam.) Nor is it enough that leadership be given simply because "he/she has so much insight into the Word!" (So does the devil.) Our society lauds and pays its athletes, entertainers and persuasive leaders just as long as they will "keep the show on the road," but that's not the measure God calls the church to apply.

Character, not merely *charisma,* is the mark of a spiritual leader, and when he or she is married, the test of that character is proven in the fabric of fidelity to vows and in the self-sacrificing will to serve marriage above ministry. To lower this expectation is too risky.

A Portent of Danger

I am persuaded by a portent of danger in our midst—of a frightening vulnerability to damning error if this bent toward neglecting the basic and practical standards God sets for leaders continues. If any continue to give place to confusion at these points, they will—*and I beg you, beware, in the name of Jesus!*—they will give place to satanic darkness that will issue in a plague of spiritual death.

This is no idle warning. The wolf is already at the door, and he's wearing sheep's clothing! Already there have been leaders duped by a demonic doctrine secretly being spread by a former "Charismatic" leader in the greater Atlanta area. One of the personalities making sad headlines due to unscriptural attitudes toward the moral and marital requirements of a spiritual leader became a willingly deceived victim of this teaching—a destructive heresy that suggests "immorality is impossible within the kingdom." I will not dignify this corruption by explaining the convolutions and distortion of Scripture that underlie this error. But it stands as contemporary evidence that there are still those who literally *teach* immorality and dilute marital commitment, exactly as the Word warns the last times shall have (1 Tim. 4:1–2).

This is precisely what Jesus Himself so forcibly opposed in the churches at Pergamos and Thyatira (Rev. 2:14, 20–25). We are wise to heed this warning, for unless the living church shakes herself awake where seducing spirits are luring her away from a "first love" for the values of marital commitment and moral fidelity, a false definition of God's Person will supplant the pure glory of His real presence and give place to destructive delusion.

So What Shall We Do?

First, heeding His Word, and with a renewed God-fearing alertness, we need to each invite, advocate and enforce a Holy Spirit-enabled recommitment to marriage standards among church leaders. In so doing, we will effectively resist the devil at this point where the infiltration of worldly marriage standards for spiritual leadership has given place to the penetration of evil destroying the foundations of Christian homes everywhere. A turnaround can be effected. Psalm

11:3 is a question containing a warning, not a cry of defeat: "If the foundations are destroyed, what can the righteous do?" Isaiah 58:12 answers, assuring us that the Lord will enable us to "raise up the foundations" again. Where the salt of the church's shepherds' influence in home and marriage may have lost its flavor, and where their sheep have followed in carelessness, our return to the Word and welcome to the Spirit's purifying can bring dynamic restoration.

Second, the issues of biblical requirements must be taught and administrated with evenhanded patience and grace, but nonetheless with faithfulness to the truth. This article is not an appeal for legalistic administration, but a call from the present sloppiness that deals "grace" in the name of "love," yet irresponsibly overlooks love's *commitments* and grace's *power.* Through true love God *lifts,* and through true grace God's *gift* enables couples to recommit to one another and to walk in God's ways by God's power. Mark the words, please: Neither love nor grace is ever a label to bandage over our neglect or self-indulgence.

Let us be done with the shallow administration of easy exits from marriage, especially when it plays leapfrog with one union in order to jump to the next.

Third, let us pray for our pastoral leaders, pursuing practical means to help strengthen and secure them in their marriages. Here are three possibilities:

- [■] Let all training for ministry leadership commit to training and shaping ministry candidates for their marriage as well as for their ministry. In God's eyes, my fidelity to my wife is as important as my integrity in handling His Word or my purity in relating to the truth it contains. All Bible schools, training centers and seminaries must become responsive to this call.

- [■] Let all Christian media accept the responsibility to monitor, minister, admonish and administrate with reference to God's standards for a leader's marriage and morality. Most networks, publishers and broadcast stations do this, but some do not...yet. By God's grace a uniform standard will be raised, showing it is not enough that a leader merely be "successful," or that they "sell," but rather that they be "found faithful" (1 Cor. 4:2).

- [■] Let all congregations, denominations and other fellowships of churches aggressively provide and fund nurturing resources for pastoral couples. It is not enough to provide "burn clinics" for those who have been wounded or fallen. There is a cry today to advance means of preventative care. New resources are rising to answer this crisis: Use them!

With such priorities pursued anew, a true visitation of miracle power can be expected. Jesus likes weddings—we know that, because He chose one for His *first* miracle. It just may be that our giving His kind of attention to our marriages—especially to His expectations for we who lead—may give place to His *final* miracle visit!

Jack Hayford, "Don't Marriage Vows Matter Anymore?" *Charisma* (February 2001): 60–68.

The Leader's Edge

This article starts with a smile—and a small boy's upset stomach. But the sickness is a paradigm for what immaturity can produce at any edge. Case in point: The quest for a competitive "edge" can lead any leader astray, looking for "something no one else has" in order to seize recognition or prominence. Among church leaders, a search for "the new" or for "God's power" is certainly appropriate, but all of God's *new* and *powerful* come on timeless and truth-rooted terms. *Gnosticism* was the name given the ancient cults that supposed a "secret knowing," which was actually nothing more than a tragic surrender to delusion under the supposition of having superior insight—"heretofore unrevealed." The "edge," for all who teach the Word of God, is simple. Just *study:* and immerse that study in prayer before God's throne.

For More...

Ask yourself the question, "What have I read recently that was classic or basic theology, something written by the proven and trusted writers of the past?"

Subscribe to *Christian History*, a highly readable, quarterly journal published by Christianity Today, Inc.[12] For a written-for-popular-use summary of basic doctrines, I offer *Grounds for Living*, which was born of my own twenty-four quantity audiocassette teaching set by the same name.

[chapter 17]

Doctrines of Demons

MY six-year-old grandson just threw up all over my office carpet!

This may not be the most noble, invigorating or spiritual thought that has come your way today, but his "moment" came pretty close to expressing my feelings just before he unloaded.

I was dutifully preparing to write my regular column—getting my thoughts together and reviewing a letter I asked a friend to send me regarding one of the subjects at hand—when my grandson (an otherwise bright, happy first-grade kid) appeared at the door.

"C'mon in," I said, opening a short conversation that began with my inquiring into how things were going at school, what new friends he was making, what studies he liked best and the like. Suddenly, a smiling mouth turned upside down, and he started to cry.

"My stomach hurts, Grandpa," and with no more warning, *splash*.

I don't think this was his response to my questions about school. He really likes school a lot. And I'm not exactly sure what spawned the splash, though I had time to guess during the next half hour of blotting, sponging, wiping and spraying. (You'd probably rather I not describe what my keen discernment assessed as source of the upset, but it wasn't hard to diagnose the source now that his dinner was clearly in evidence.)

He cried. I comforted him and took him into the bathroom to stand in front of the toilet in case of an encore. Thankfully he had apparently plumbed his whole system in one gush, because there were no further "visitations." I was glad, naturally, and my only regret for the whole evening (though I was sorry for the little guy) was that he wasn't downstairs in the den where his Grandma Anna was when he struck pay dirt. That would have been her domain and would have allowed me to remain silently "at work" in my office while she tended the mess.

Sick, Sick, Sick

I mused over this transient event as I washed my hands and shoes and deposited my socks and slacks in the washer. (I told you above—his shot was "all over," only slightly less than the one "heard 'round the world.") As I did, I was suddenly comforted myself; struck with the feeling that there was possibly something peculiarly providential in my grandson's eruption; something almost "prophetic," if you will. (Note: I pause to assure "whoever" that I didn't *really* think his outburst was prophetic, since there *are* a few wild-eyed saints ever ready to attribute *some* spiritual meaning to virtually *anything* that happens.) Anyway, though I'm not attributing spiritual meaning to my/his minor ordeal, I will say that the subject of my column is loaded with *sick, sick, sick* ideas. To some degree, they are enough to crowd me toward the edge of repeating my grandson's performance myself.

My "subject" (bet you thought I'd never get to it!) is Twenty-first Century Gnosticism—a pretty august theme for a column that begins with curds and whey. I am upset—really! Because in the last few weeks I've come across two of the most disgusting, nauseatingly unbiblical ideas I've encountered in forty years of ministry, both presented as *revelations*—"insightful, heretofore unperceived secrets only now perceptible to the truly mature."

Bizarre…Bizarre!

The first had to do with marriage, or rather, with "not really being married at all, even when you are." (Try that on for starters!)

The concept advanced was a bizarre twist on "kingdom teaching" that argued that once a person has entered the kingdom he transcends earth's order and is thereby exempt from its laws. Even from God's laws. Being "beyond" the mundane requirements of morality, the proposition blithely declared, "We are now outside the possibility of committing adultery!" (Hold on, it gets worse.)

In this system, this "incapacity to sin" has nothing to do with being freed *from* sin, but with being free to do things that *used to be* sin until the "kingdom person" entered his or her new, enlightened state. Then sexual disobedience (that old idea contained in God's Holy Word) becomes *passé,* since no such thing as "infidelity" exists any longer. Whatever ensues in sexual indulgence with however many partners a person pleases becomes redefined as some exalted state of spiritual interaction and mutual ministry to one another. (I always thought you called this a "free-love cult," but I guess I'm just not mature enough to capture the depths of it all.)

The second "bizarre" notion had to do with demons—well, not quite "demons," but actually "human spirits" that, at death, were somehow pirated away by demonic beings before they could make it to heaven or hell. Now, being subject to the spirits that captured them, they are often transmitted to living humans who experience a unique spiritual bondage. This isn't the usual kind that involves the possibility of deliverance by means of something so unoriginal as casting the evil spirit out in the name of Jesus. In fact (talk about "good news"), these "demons" might even be led to accept Jesus as Lord and be ushered *out* of the person they inhabit and *into* heaven! Of course, they might not accept Him, so the alternative of hell also exists if they refuse the counsel of the "minister" seeking to bring "deliverance" to the person victimized by this bondage.

Give me a massive break! No wonder sound-minded deliverance ministries have a hard time gaining a hearing! (And by the way, did I mention that many of the above "insights" were gained while those propagating this idiocy were talking with the demons who explained this to them?)

Anyone Have a Bible Handy?

The horror of all this nonsense is that *anyone* believes it—that is, anyone who is anywhere within five miles of a Bible. It's there—*there* in God's Word we are warned "that in latter times some will depart from the faith, giving heed to deceiving spirits and *doctrines of demons,* speaking lies in hypocrisy, having their own conscience seared with a hot iron, forbidding to marry…" (1 Tim. 4:1-3, emphasis added). Jesus Himself indicts two churches with the evil of hearing false teachers who "hold the doctrine of Balaam…[who] *teach and seduce My servants* to commit sexual immorality" (Rev. 2:14, 20, emphasis added).

Of course, there are a host of other passages God's Word affords, any one of which will expose and explode the evils indulged here. But desperate people listen, "for the time will come when they will not endure sound doctrine, but according to their own desires, because they have itching ears, they will heap up for themselves teachers; and they will turn their ears away from the truth, and be turned aside to fables" (2 Tim. 4:3-4).

So it is, faithful pastor-servant. It isn't merely the kooks who are on the loose, but there are "sickies" still rampant in this century as in the first. The apostles faced the same order of false teachers then, and they haven't gone away. They still sally forth, sowing tares in patches of kingdom terrain, marketing their weeds like dope peddlers, selling fallacy as a "new high"—an advanced revelation beyond what others know or can grasp. Thus they license their corrupt pursuit of self-indulgence and leverage themselves into a position of manipulative control over the ignorant.

What to Do?

Thank you for sitting with me in the aftermath of my descriptive opening to this column. (If you survived that, my guess is that by now—if you feel as I do about all this—you're probably near-ready to join my grandson's performance.)

What can we do? Really, just one thing. "Preach the word! Be ready in season and out of season. Convince, rebuke, exhort, with all longsuffering and teaching" (2 Tim. 4:2). Yessir! Just "hold forth the faithful Word," and keep feeding your flock as a good shepherd. I don't think there's reason to spend a lot of time elaborating the sordid details behind these twisted notions of presumed arcane insight.

In fact, I wouldn't bother to take this much time with it, except there *are* times you have to mop up the vomit some-body donated.

Jack Hayford, "Doctrines of Demons," *Ministries Today* (November/December 2000): 18–19.

The Leader's Edge

Some are making an issue today of this article's question. Thoughtful leaders will stand firm on solid authority—the Bible endorses two-way personal communication with God! There is nothing more fundamental to wise leadership than seeking God for direction, protection and correction. The Bible is the central and ultimately authoritative source for such confirmation, but its objective authority was never meant to supplant the subjective intimacy of God's personal guidance to individuals. God's Word is filled with examples, and He is still speaking today. This article was written to confront doubts being sown by a few leaders who suppose the Bible is dishonored when the Holy Spirit's voice is listened to. Let leaders rise who *seek* God, *hear* from God and *obey* God—all according to His Word.

For More...

One of the most thoroughgoing, biblically sound works on this subject has been written by noted international Bible teacher Joy Dawson. This respected leader of proven wisdom and godliness has made a remarkable contribution to all of us in her book *Forever Ruined for the Ordinary*.[13]

[chapter 18]

Does God Speak Today?

PARDON my bluntness, but I'm really getting tired of hearing respected evangelicals attack anyone who says, "The Lord spoke to me." There's been a growing body of verbiage today debunking the idea that God speaks personally to people anymore. Whatever the warning value about kooks, I'm disturbed because these attacks seek to ban a biblical, privileged expectation of the redeemed and also level wholesale assaults on *anyone* who claims "a word from the Lord" or that God spoke to them in the privacy of their own walk with Him.

First, let me shout it: *Yes, God's Word is absolute authority!* I don't know any spiritually alive or reasonably alert Christian—Charismatic or non—who *ever* thinks otherwise. Whatever demographic studies may regrettably report of "Christians" who live according to their own subjective or relativistic values, they don't represent me, and I doubt they represent you. In fact, in the broad circles of my familiarity, I find that experienced Pentecostal/Charismatic leadership is pretty consistent in confronting weird and wandering opinions of spiritually muddled souls. Still, increasing criticism is black-listing all of us who receive "words" of prophecy by the Holy Spirit or describe an encounter with the Lord as though He spoke with us. What can be said to hopefully set this matter at rest—and what place does God's Word give to the subject?

God Has Been Speaking

Since critics argue that "God only speaks today through the Bible," let's turn there first and see what it reveals about "the voice of God." To do so is to immediately be forced to won-der that anyone would resist the idea that God reveals Himself to humankind in many ways—including speaking directly to individuals and groups. From history's beginning, God has been and still is speaking in at least seven ways.

1. **He speaks through creation's glory, artistry and majesty with such clarity that the Bible says all humankind is held accountable to believe in the Creator on these grounds alone. (See Psalm 19:1-6; Romans 1:20.)**

2. **He speaks through the moral sense placed in the human conscience, so that a fundamental sense of right and wrong is innately present, and that on these grounds God may exercise judgment. (See Romans 2:14-15.)**

3. **He speaks through the evidences of divine providence that affect our lives and speak to our souls, often caus-ing humans to respond with wonder, wisdom, grati-tude or repentance. (See Genesis 28:10-17; Acts 16:7.)**

4. He speaks through signs and wonders or prophecies prompted by the Holy Spirit (including tongues with interpretation), by these means edifying believers and often convincing unbelievers of His power and presence. (See 2 Kings 2:15; Acts 13:12; 1 Corinthians 14:5, 22-26.)

5. He speaks by His "still small voice," addressing people within their hearts, speaking with personal assurance, correction, insight or guidance by His own express choice to do so. (See 1 Kings 11:12; Isaiah 30:21; Acts 10:9-12.)

6. He speaks through His authoritative Word, the inspired and inerrant Holy Scriptures, which He has given through His prophets and apostles by the Holy Spirit in the Old and New Testament. (See 2 Timothy 3:14-17; 2 Peter 1:19-21.)

7. He has spoken finally and redemptively through His Son Jesus Christ, the living Word, who revealed the Father's heart of love to us and has become our only way of salvation for returning to Him. (See Hebrews 1:1-4; John 14:1-12.)

The evidence of God's Word is that He is always reaching and speaking, always seeking to touch and embrace, as well as to teach and correct. Seeing these several ways, however, only reminds us again of the Bible's authority in every facet of our judgment on this issue:

[■] First, we only *know* that we may *believe* God speaks to

people in these ways, and that they are spiritually valid, *because the Bible says so.*

[■] **Second, the only** *measure* **through which we may** *perceive* **what we hear God say by these means, is through** *the Bible's full teaching and authority.*

In other words, what He says by *any* means must be judged in the light of an *absolute* means—that *absolute,* of course, is the *whole Bible.*

These principles ought to settle the issue. The fear of exaggerating the relative importance of "what God said to me," or of falling into deception via any "word" or spirit, is dispensed as each believer is settled on the issue of avoiding, indeed of rejecting, any ideas of "continuing revelation." Those words address the fallacious idea that the Bible isn't the final authority concerning God's revealed will and truth. However, the Bible *is* the final authority on all life's foundational and ultimate issues, and anyone arguing otherwise should not be regarded; any Christian leader arguing otherwise should be confronted.

But with those points of control, there is still *nothing* in the Bible that justifies the position of anyone who denies the biblical grounds for God speaking to people today. Nor is there any biblical justification for anyone who declares that those of us who say things God has spoken to us are thereby embracers of error. Two well-known anti-Charismatic writers (both of whom call me a friend, for which I'm thankful) still categorize everyone who says, "God spoke to me," as a person who believes in the fallacy of "continuing revelation" or "extra-biblical revelation" (they named me as one of these, too). Of course, they are wrong about me and wrong about most Charismatics I know. And while we are talking "extra-biblical," we might assert that *it's extra-biblical to teach that God doesn't speak to His people today,* since the Bible is full of instances of God speaking to people!

Further, the Bible uses the word *revelation* in a dual sense, and as long as they are clearly understood, let the nitpicking over the use of that word be stopped. In Ephesians 1:17–18, the apostle's prayer for "the spirit of wisdom and revelation" to enlighten the hearts of believers indicates that God does "reveal" things to His children today. Such "revelation" is never to be equated with the equivalent of the *closed canon of the Scriptures*—words that refer to our clear understanding that the Bible is a *finished* book. But such "revelation" ought to be welcomed as the Holy Spirit brings the truths of His Word alive and ignites faith to embrace the Father's purposes for us (vv. 19–23).

The implications of the issue are clear:

- **The revelation of the Scriptures is final: There are not, nor ever will be, any other books, verses or ideas to be added to the Bible or placed beside it as equal in authority or revelation.**
- **All preaching, teaching, prophesying or any other communication (or *revelation*) is to be subject to measurement and judgment by the content in the eternal Word of God—the Bible.**

I Thought We All Started Here

Settling that, I should think the biblical doorway should be left open to expecting God may speak to any one of us at any time. Why not? This was where we all started, anyhow. Whatever testimony any of us bear, our story begins somehow, somewhere, when, in some way, God "spoke" to us. And while it took His Word to clarify the Way, the Truth and the Life, the fact is that there have been innumerable ways God has spoken to people in drawing them to Himself—including *speaking words* to them.

Moreover, in asking that honesty prevail with *both* what the Scriptures *say* and what the Holy Spirit has *done* in drawing many of us to Christ, let's admit that the expectation of "God talking with me" has been celebrated in all the church for ages. His personal presence, speaking to us in our daily walk, has been unapologetically acknowledged and has found a frequent place in the hymns sung by the people of the Lord. Among classic, widely sung examples in this century is:

> **I come to the garden alone, while the dew is still on the roses;**
>
> **And the voice I hear, falling on my ear, the Son of God discloses.**
>
> **And He walks with me, and He talks with me, and He tells me I am His own;**
>
> **And the joy we share as we tarry there none other has ever known.**[14]

So why has this rash of criticism lifted its head? Why speak against or attempt to intimidate sincere, Bible-centered believers and accuse us of carelessness about God's Word just because we say we hear His voice? I think I know. But it's another subject entirely, and I'll save it for another day. But for today, let it be settled—God still speaks in all the same ways He always has. He is the changeless God, and His reach to humankind continually extends by every communicative means, including His intimately speaking with His own sons and daughters in Christ by the Holy Spirit.

Jack Hayford, "God Still Speaks," *Ministries Today* (January/February 2001): 20–21.

The Leader's Edge

The broad scope of "the church at worship" is so grand a subject it seems almost to trivialize any facet of the matter with a small article. Nonetheless, I lift up a plea in the brief article that follows. Today's Christian leader—filling any role whatsoever—must *think* about worship, *grow* in worship and use his or her leadership to *advance* worship. It will take leaders "thinking through" to neutralize the toxic, remove the hazardous and bring spiritual purity and dynamic into hearts—and into the sanctuary.

For More...

Inquire into the resources of Lamar Boschman's The Worship Institute for training resources and conference information.[15] *Worship His Majesty* was my offering to the body of Christ over ten years ago.[16] Its timelessness in truth and teaching appears to be verified by the fact it still continues to find an audience. Matching video resources provide this tool for use by congregations, worship teams, choirs or individuals—making available a means for keeping the *real* in pure focus when we worship His Majesty, King Jesus.[17]

[chapter 19] Hazardous Substances—Toxic Worship?

I'M getting nervous about the worship life of the church. After watching decades of expanding renewal in adoration, exaltation and praise to the Lord, I see a setback looming on the horizon unless we're alert.

May I invite you to examine the signs and take action with me?

This past year, I have encountered with increasing frequency signs of deterioration in the worship life and practice of churches. There are "hazardous substances" that can toxify the spirit of worship if they aren't sensitively removed. What most concerns me is that I've witnessed these signs at even those places known for their influence in *advancing* the ministry of worship over the years.

Of course, I'm not given to critiquing or evaluating worship every time I enter a church, and in none of these situations did I feel a total absence of righteous worship. "Ichabod" wasn't even close to being written over the door.

I ask you to join me in taking a hard look at these potential toxins in the life of my own congregation. You might want to check out yours.

1. Firm Up the Slack Regarding Worship's Priority

Worship transcends an individual department or ministry within your congregation. It touches your church's soul. What transpires in the worship life of an assembly is precisely parallel to what takes place in the communication of a married couple. Healthy interaction in a marriage brings clarity of understanding, harmony of agreement, mutuality in goals, peace in the home and fulfillment in intimacy. You and I need to lead the bride of Christ to become rightly tuned for worshiping her Lord. When the spirit of pure worship abounds, harmonized hearts find "agreeing" power in prayer, the will of the Father is discerned in churchwide pursuits, the local family is happy together and a life-begetting spirit of evangelism breeds a multiplication of souls.

2. Beware of an Increasing Takeover of the "Performance Syndrome"

Perhaps the greatest thing that has happened in the renewal of worship has been the restoration of worship to the *whole* congregation—everyone entering in, every voice lifted, all heads and hands turned heavenward. It's been thrilling, and it's been right! In many cases, choirs and instruments that had become a substitute for a congregation's strong involvement were dismissed for a season. The renewal didn't "kill" choral music, but we did discover that too many people in too many congregations were letting the choir take their place.

Unwittingly, a host of churches had become performance-oriented in worship—allowing the congregation's role to shift from praising God with a "new song" to observing a handful of the more gifted do it for them. And as is often the case when this syndrome sets in, people had begun to give more attention to judging or scoring the performance of the "substitutes" than to entering into the spirit of worship themselves. The renewal changed that—for a time.

I visited two outstanding churches recently and was greatly blessed at both. Yet I was concerned to find evidence of a slow but sure retreat to the performance syndrome, obvious from the moment the worship teams—both gifted and godly in style—took the platform. Because I was unfamiliar with the local repertoires, I mostly listened, singing as often as I could when verses were repeated. And while I listened, I looked around, observing people without gawking at them. *In both places, on virtually all the songs, no more than half to two-thirds of the people were singing.* Ever.

The nonparticipating ones weren't passive. They watched steadfastly, glanced at the projected lyrics occasionally, smiled pleasantly at times—all in all, they weren't irreverent. But they were *spectators.* And the more I analyzed the situations later, the more I realized that "spectatorship" is an *immediate* liability.

Though the musicians and vocalists were not ostentatious or visibly detracting from worship in any carnal way, they were excellent. Now that can hardly be faulted. But because they were so good, rather than actually drawing the whole body into praiseful worship, they became more of a "concert."

The performance syndrome creeps in wherever passivity is produced, however unintentionally. What began in renewal with *simple* worship teams simply leading *beautiful worship* has now become, in many places, *beautiful worship teams* trying to lead *simpler* people (musically speaking). Giftedness can unwittingly quench, and skilled complexity will surely overturn simplicity's best efforts.

Thoughtful leaders will take a look at this challenge and

take steps to keep us on track—with beauty being sustained in worship through the stimulating of the whole body to praise. None of us want to succumb to a syndrome that allows "substitutes" for our individual entries into full-hearted worship before the Father's throne.

3. Watch Out for "Corrosive Casualness"

I don't have a problem with casual dress or an informal style in church. But there is a difference between informality and slothfulness. I'll make this point brief because I don't want to sound snobbish. In my travels I've noted—among leaders as well as those being led—a virtual sanctification of indifference. This isn't necessarily shown in the music or musicians (although that has been the case at times). But this deterrent to the spirit of worship is found in everything from obviously unplanned services to a meandering style that wanders from point to point in the meeting until there is no point at all.

I'm not arguing for a regimented, drilled attack on services. Nor am I requiring ties and suits for men and billowing dresses and gaudy hats for women. But if I as a leader fail to perceive the relationship between certain disciplines of habit, dress and preparation, and the matter of discipleship in Christ, a deadly corrosiveness can take over my congregation.

We live in a declining society that increasingly disrespects any expectations placed upon it. And what we model as congregations-at-worship is, in many cases, all the "ordered living" to which some of our people are ever exposed. Thus, I believe we have a challenge to do more than merely mirror a worldly sloppiness or slothfulness that travels in the guise of "casual." There's a difference, and in each of our cultural settings I believe the Holy Spirit will help us as leaders to discern it—if we're tuned to the need for such discernment.

4. Let's Not Lose Our Capacity for Grandeur

This isn't a continuation of the preceding point. I'm addressing the grandeur of God—not a grandness of human style. Let us pursue Him in all His holiness—not for the production of religious prudes, but for the healing of human beings.

Worship by definition is "to ascribe worth." And while our praise is ideally to be focused on magnifying *God's* worthiness, the fact is that this is not a one-way street. When you or I attribute worth to Him, the impact of that worship inevitably rebounds and pours fresh worth into us as well. That's what the psalmist means when he asserts that worshipers become like the deity they adore. (See Psalm 115:3–8.)

CUTTING TO THE CORE—FACING LEADERSHIP ISSUES...

Check the lyrics of the twenty most-sung songs from your recent worship services. How often do the words *holy* or *worthy* occur? Now please, I'm not on a lyrical witch hunt. But I do want to point out that those are the two key themes that, according to Scripture, throb from the songs sung around the throne of God. Obviously, they aren't the only appropriate themes for praise and worship, but they are the two foundational ones. And if their thread is not sustained in the fabric of our worship, the garments of praise will eventually wear thin—or disintegrate.

I'm not intending to provoke a flood of letters challenging my right to assert ultimate worship values and styles, because I'm neither claiming that role nor declaring "ultimates" of any kind. But I think I'm on track with a warning from the Holy Spirit. We are just as vulnerable as any renewal in history to the loss of our vital life signs. Worship renewal has been a paramount feature of our era, and only seasonally revitalized worship will maintain its true power.

Jack Hayford, "Of Thanksgiving, Praise and Angel Song," *Ministries Today* (November/December 1992): 22–23.

The Leader's Edge

Church leaders either receive salaries, influence salaries or both. The mandates of Scripture are clearer than many will acknowledge, and there is no way the issue of spiritually wise, biblically righteous management dare be neglected. This article was heralded by many when it first appeared. At the same time, I know of at least one leader who broke fellowship with me because of it. He didn't say that was his reason—he simply stopped "showing up." Today his ministry is sadly discredited. Sadder still is this fact: Inconsistency in financial management usually paves a trail to other errors— be it doctrinal confusion, prideful arrogance, moral compromise or marital failure. Clear thinking on clergy salaries eventually will *always* have to do with more than money.

For More...

I strongly believe it is God's will that spiritual leaders be graciously supported, and that stingy church administrators who do otherwise block divinely intended channels of blessing to the local congregation and its people. But I also believe that the leader is to lead in giving—not merely in teaching as much. Biblical principles of giving faithfully taught *and lived* by the leader will release abundance for all involved. Shortly after its release, John Maxwell referred to my book *The Key to Everything* as the best book he had read on financial stewardship.[18] That affirmation encourages my mention of it here as a sourcebook for leaders regarding finance.

[chapter 20] Questions About Clergy Salaries

GOD'S Word offers three important principles about how much money a minister should make. When it comes to church finances, one of the most common questions I encounter is this: What amount of compensation do you believe is appropriate for a pastor's salary? As often as not, it's a question asked by pastors themselves. Most leaders I know are concerned about this—not in a self-serving way, but with a concern for being equitable and ethical when it comes to their income.

This is especially true when a congregation experiences healthy or even phenomenal growth—with a proportional increase of responsibility being borne by its leaders. The question is a natural in that context: How much of a church's increase should be apportioned to its leadership? Is the church's success to be administrated like that of a secular corporation, with "rewards" being given to the executives who were "key" to its success? Or is the fruitfulness of a church presumed to be the manifestation of God's grace alone, making the undue acknowledgment of any individual's role an act of idolatry?

Avoiding the Stereotypes

Certainly there exists an appropriate place where the labor of effective leaders is honored with increase, even as those to whom they minister enjoy the blessing of God through their gifts. Still, it will usually befall the leaders themselves to establish the mood and to secure the parameters by which salary distribution is made—especially their own.

As *servants* in the church, godly leaders should be more inclined to guard against excess, however lovingly intended by those who advise toward exaggerated generosity. I lament cases where I have found leaders who yield to the ill-advised counsel of any who urge them to accept lavish treatment. This is an idolatrous practice in some circles, and not at all worthy even though it may be socially acceptable in a given culture.

But by and large, despite media image-shaped reports of worst-case scenarios of self-indulgence, most pastors and other gospel ministers are, at best, only average, middle-class wage earners. Virtually none of them are interested in "lining their pockets" at the expense of their flocks—yet unfortunately, the qualifier "virtually none" must be acknowledged.

I was disappointed recently at the public disclosure made by a renowned friend, whose exorbitant from-the-ministry-income flew in the face of counsel he had earlier asked for and received from peers, including myself. Such cases work against the health of the church in at least two ways:

- **They intensify the vulnerability of those who might be tempted to capitalize on increased ministry success. The "poverty spirit" seeks to snare us all with illusions of wealth as the secret to our security or the just rewards of our labor.**
- **They justify the world's suspicion that the church is no different from the world—that it is money-driven and engineered by leaders who are motivated by carnal quests for their own creature comforts at the expense of those they are able to manipulate.**

Of course, there are aboundingly more worthy cases of leaders who model a humble spirit of sacrifice and service through their non-self-seeking approach to remuneration. Further, there are many whose devotion to ministry is never reduced though they are paid very little. Low salaries are generally due to the limited resources of small congregations; however, they too often represent an inequity administrated at the hands of controlling, ungrateful boards indifferent to the biblical salary directives that not only limit excessiveness but also prohibit stinginess. (Incidentally, my above reference to "from-the-ministry-income" is to separate what a pastor or leader is compensated from any other income they may receive apart from his or her ministry—such as inheritances, the fruit of former business enterprises, investments, royalties and so on.)

Three Prerequisites From God's Word

God's Word, of course, is our sourcebook and point of final counsel, and it doesn't take a brilliant mind to settle three issues on this subject:

1. Support is required.

First Timothy 5:17 is clear: "Let the elders who rule well be counted worthy of double honor, especially those who labor in the word and doctrine." This text is a mandatory call for those who receive ministry from teachers and preachers to see their responsibility to support the ministers as a divinely assigned charge.

It includes a recommendation to be generous: "Let...double honor..." The "double honor" is subject to interpretation, possibly meaning simply the "two-way" honor of financial support and the personal, respectful acknowledgment of the congregation. But "double honor" may also suggest a "double" level of income.

This "double" concept seems to indicate that a spiritual leader's role should parallel, in salary, a person of executive status in the local community. The truth is that, applied in conjunction with other biblical guidelines, such a "doubling" has limits—it should never exceed an approximate "two times" the average income in the community being served. Such generosity, where possible, is not to enrich, but to enable, allowing a leader to pursue ministry without being distracted by financial concerns, and can also allow him or her to show added generosity and hospitality to others.

The doubling concept strikes at the core of any vain (to my view) supposition that the pastor-leader's salary should automatically be commensurate with some percentage of the congregation's income. I believe it also undercuts any system that generates systematic (as opposed to special occasion) "love offerings" that exploit the affection of people to the enrichment of the leader.

2. Acquisitiveness is prohibited.

"Not greedy for money" is a recurrent phrase in the

required personal qualifications for spiritual leaders. (See 1 Timothy 3:3, 8; Titus 1:7.) Furthermore, warnings against a leader's becoming subtly motivated by income potential to manipulate money matters in an opportunistic way are plentiful. (See 2 Timothy 3:1-2; 1 Peter 5:2.) Revelation 2:14, while not directly mentioning Balaam's greed, strongly suggests the dangerous link between this sin and the sin of sexual immorality—offenses that too often go together when leaders fall.

3. Restraint is modeled.

An honest handling of the whole Word of God clearly demonstrates a balanced approach to a spiritual leader's income and possessions. Nowhere does it require we who lead to take an oath of poverty (though I honor any who submit to such a sense of mission for their own lives). But the call of Christ is clearly one to a life of discipline—one that calls me to a full removal from any preoccupation with my income, possessions or material resources. (See Matthew 6:24-34.)

Frankly, "removal from economic preoccupation" is what I believe is at the root of the concept of providing "double honor" to a leader. The purpose isn't enrichment, but sufficient provision to keep economic strain "off the back" of a leader. That way, money never becomes preoccupying—either its lack or its undue abundance.

Straining Scripture

But there is another issue to be resolved, because there is an insidious capacity of our flesh to find means to justify any of its unworthy quests. In this regard, few of us are unaware of the strained textual arguments that some have advanced in order to prove "Jesus was rich, and Paul was affluent." The bottom-line facts remain unchanged: Jesus, the Son of Man, had "nowhere to lay His head." (See Matthew 8:20.) He was buried in a borrowed grave. Paul worked that he might not be a burden to any of those to whom he ministered. (See 1 Thessalonians 2:9.)

Yes, I have heard the apostle's words in Philippians 4:18 yanked from their context and used to justify a leader's personal enrichment ("abounding"). And I've heard this proposition elaborated to infer that offerings that enrich a leader are "well pleasing to God." However, two things argue conclusively against such a materialistic interpretation.

The first is the immediate context, which indicates that Paul honored the Philippians' "sacrifice" because it reflected their own spiritual devotion to God (Phil. 4:18). It also demonstrated the increasing spiritual fruitfulness in their lives (v. 17).

Second, Philippians 4:15–17 reveals that the apostle did absolutely nothing to generate this financial show of love, and it gives us a chronological context. His mention of being in Thessalonica when receiving an earlier gift tells us that the Philippian offering came at a time when Paul was already gainfully employed in secular work by his own choice. (See 1 Thessalonians 2:9–12.)

While Paul saw financial income and support as a rightful privilege for a spiritual leader from those he or she served, there is nothing to argue that he ever saw "abundance" as meaning "acquisitiveness." (See 1 Thessalonians 2:6; 1 Corinthians 9:3–11.) In Philippians 4, the "abounding" he references was not the sole result of the offering from Philippi—it was the joint sum of their gift added to his secularly earned income. Further, from other counsel he gives, we know the apostle never saw a believer's abundance as self-focused. In Ephesians 4:28, he shows income as a means of ministering with one's gain, not simply acquiring wealth for oneself.

If I as a leader ever use the people I serve as a means of increasing my own profit at their expense, I've succumbed to "money-grubbing." If my identification with the need in my flock is contradicted by excessiveness manifest in my own possessions, I've submitted to "flamboyancy." The car I drive, the clothes I wear, the accessories surrounding me, my general lifestyle traits—all these must be carefully measured with the Scriptures and the spirit they reveal, with my own heart of shapeable, correctable integrity before God, and through my submittedness to peers who will confront me if necessary.

In the last analysis, spiritual leaders will usually be the masters of their own financial fates. God alone can bless—but we are assigned to manage. And self-management and self-control will ever and always be a challenge and a responsibility we must accept.

With forty years of ministry behind me, I think I understand a little of Paul's words, "I know how to be abased, and I know how to abound" (Phil. 4:12). Both have proved joyous. But I have also learned that a tight rein must be kept on "abundance" lest my call to model the servant-spirit of biblical leadership ever be compromised.

Jack Hayford, "Questions About Clergy Salaries," *Ministries Today* (September/October 1997): 25–26, 76.

The Leader's Edge

There is a tendency against a church leader's being willing to stand firmly on biblical, Christ-modeled ground concerning the ministry of healing. I present this issue for the obvious reasons—sickness, affliction and suffering have not gone away, but neither has the presence of the living Christ, who said, "These signs will follow those who believe...they will lay hands on the sick, and they will recover" (Mark 16:17-18). We are called to reach with this expression of God's love—and called to anticipate instances of confirming grace. Healings and miracles are promised—we just don't know when or where, and we are called to offer the possibility, not the guarantee. The promise is God's. The privilege (and responsibility) to proclaim it is ours.

For More...

Dr. Nathaniel Van Cleave was my theology professor in "Healing" over forty years ago. He is still alive at ninety-four years of age (August 2001) *and preaching!* His Kingdom Dynamics articles, though only twenty-four brief presentations on the theme "The Ministry of Divine Healing," are some of the most effective biblical summaries of this truth I have seen.[19]

[chapter 21] A Climate of Love... Extending a Grace

IT'S not a matter of choice. The ministry of healing in the local church is a primary leadership responsibility for those of us who pastor.

The *climate* for healing is developed and sustained where the love of God is pronouncedly declared and demonstrated. It rises with solid teaching and is released when we recognize that it's only our call to extend the grace of God and the truth of His Word regarding the ministry of healing. We aren't called to *defend* the Word, but to *declare* it. Unbelief feeds on defensiveness—that sense of needing to protect God from "failing" someone's expectations. Once I submit to that burden, I will cease to foster boldness among the congregation in praying for the sick, and I will be inclined toward withdrawal myself.

At our church, the *time* and *place* for healing is provided through a Personal Ministry Room. It's open following every service and staffed by people prepared to counsel and to pray about problems, healing, deliverance or the fullness of the Spirit.

As a means of *consistent pursuit* of healing, I also like to periodically place a "healing statement" before the people. It gives them something to study and think about, something around which to develop roots. Perhaps mine will help you frame your own—or declare the same yourself.

I Believe in God's Will to Heal

I believe it is God's will to heal and deliver the sick and the tormented, and that He has revealed the fullness of His healing purpose in His Son, Jesus Christ. I believe it is in God's nature to work redemptively to heal by every possible means, inasmuch as His mercy and loving-kindness are ever open to provide grace for the relief of human need, pain, misery and sin.

Because I believe this, I offer praise to the Creator who has made all things well, affirming that all sickness and pain is adverse to His will and desire for mankind, and has only come upon the race because of mankind's fallen state. I declare thanksgiving to Him for the fact that—notwithstanding every effort of hell to steal, kill and destroy all of mankind, compounded by human weakness and vulnerability to pain, sickness, disease, deformity and tragedy—the Father has appointed multiple havens of refuge from sickness and pain: through natural recuperative processes; through climate and diet; through the charitable efforts of mankind; through hospitals, doctors and medicine; and through the divine means of healing gifts distributed by the Holy Spirit and ministered in the name of Jesus.

I believe in the power of Jesus Christ to heal the sick and afflicted, and to break any bondage of satanic sort when His name is invoked in any circumstance. I believe His power is as consistently available today as it was during His own earthly ministry, and that through His cross He has provided the grounds for us to expect and receive healing and deliverance as surely as we may receive forgiveness and sanctification.

Because I believe this, I accept the ministry of healing as a part of the Lord Jesus Christ's commission that the church go to the whole world with the gospel. I proclaim God's will and power to heal; and in Jesus' name, I instruct that the prayer of faith be offered, that confession of sins be made unto deliverance, that elders anoint with oil and that hands be laid on the sick that they may recover.

I believe in the power of God's Word and Spirit to sustain and supply health when believers walk simply and humbly before Him in faith. I believe the fruit of such faith will be manifest in love and patience, and so I correspondingly reject any system that begets lovelessness or induces guilt when a believer in Jesus does not seem to be able to receive physical healing or personal deliverance from sickness or any other torment.

Because I believe this, I withstand every evidence of pain, suffering, sickness, disease, bondage or torment, convinced that the good fight of faith will prevail unto health. I am equally convinced that in any case where victory is not evidenced, that a victory of another order is being realized by the divine grace of Almighty God.

With such faith as this, I move in the ministry of prayer, faith and healing, so that Jesus Christ is glorified and, in all circumstances, His church is edified.[20]

Jack Hayford, "The Pastor's Role in Divine Healing," *Ministries Today* (January/February 1991): 28.

CUTTING TO THE CORE—FACING LEADERSHIP ISSUES...

The Leader's Edge

Unlike most the articles in this book, this one presumes a "Charismatic church" context. My forty-plus years of pastoral service have always been in an environment where Paul's words in 1 Corinthians 14 were taken seriously. The apostle emphasized "prophecy" (which was clearly the prompting of the Holy Spirit giving people words of "exhortation, edification or comfort" to give to others). He also gave clear instruction as to how prophecy's exercise in a vital, vibrant congregation was to be governed. In short, it was nothing of an "anything goes" sort of thing—a casual, if not reckless, style not uncommon in many Charismatic groups today. Accordingly, this is an issue that calls for leadership emboldened by God's Word and willing to teach, lead and govern in ways to retain both order and freedom in the body.

For More...

For over thirty years, welcoming the exercise of "the gift of prophecy" has been neither a diversion, distraction or delusion in the congregation I serve at The Church On The Way. Biblical principles that have guided, kept and profited us are elaborated in three audiocassette teachings, "How to Receive Prophesyings." This companions with "The Plea for Prophesying" to form a quartet of teaching expanding beyond the basics in the accompanying article. *The Gift of Prophecy in the New Testament and Today* is also an excellent resource.[21]

[chapter 22]

Despise Not Prophesyings

HOW do you handle "prophecies" given to you or spoken to your flock?

I've had situations tempt me to despise prophecies. How about you? So many lives have been shredded by misguided or manipulative "words from the Lord." So many church services have been divided by a veil of confusion—all because of a prophetic "word." No wonder Paul had to warn against "despising prophesying" (1 Thess. 5:20).

Harper's Greek Lexicon defines *exoutheneo (despise)* as "to make light of, to set at naught, to treat or reject with scorn." In short, the apostle's command prohibits anything that would *mock, deride* or *cheapen* the place of prophecy.

In this sense, prophecy is a means by which several members may participate in a service, prompted by the Holy Spirit to relate ideas or thoughts—"a word"—that may edify, exhort or comfort. It is *a word,* always to be based upon and measured by *the Word.*

As a pastor, I need to:

[■] *Deliver* prophetic "words" God gives me.
[■] *Respond* to those "words" ministered from the assembly.
[■] *Integrate* vital "words" into the body-life.

How can I release this gift's blessing without confusion?

I was speaking to a gathering of churches in one city recently when suddenly a prophecy boomed forth. I listened carefully, first to hear the content, second to sense the response of the mixed crowd—many of whom were unaccustomed to such utterances. The ill-conceived "word" absolutely quenched the strong spirit of prayer upon the group.

Looking around, I winced in noting the man who was sounding forth as the "voice of God." I not only knew him (a sincere soul), but years ago I was his pastor. I remember the delicate line I sought to walk, trying to help release his gifting and teach him balance and discipline in its exercise. He clearly had forgotten those lessons, and though the meeting wasn't ruined, it was anything but helped.

I went to him later asking why he hadn't first submitted the word to the leaders of the meeting. He bluntly replied, "I did what the Lord told me to do!"

Had he? I don't think so.

First Corinthians 14:26-40 gives clear instruction on how the Spirit's gift of prophecy can be ministered *and* administered. The teaching is that a prophecy (that is, a truth God wants to remind us about or encourage us with) is to be judged. This means to evaluate it, to weigh what has been said in the light of the Bible's teaching and so determine the place the message fits in the flow of a service. It also includes application—what ought to be done in response to the insight the "word" brings. (I lament the glib habit of applauding prophetic words as though the whole idea of the gift were to excite us.)

In my early ministry, I was uncertain how to welcome prophesying without inviting problems. Then I was introduced to the concept of "submitting the 'word.'" By *submitting*, I mean that anyone feeling God has given them a "word" first present the gist of the message to an elder. I believe this is as valid a fulfillment of the apostolic directive to judge the prophecy as if we waited until it is given publicly.

At first I wondered if this practice might obstruct the liberty of the Spirit, but instead I found it *released* ministry. Individuals sensing the Spirit's prompting with a word were liberated, and the congregation seemed freer to receive. This custom removed the person's appearing to be seizing the service at his or her own discretion. Members of the body learn to trust eldership who assist the release of the gifting within the assembly. Thus, when during a worship segment of the service a member submits a word to an elder, our goal is to see that "word" ministered, not to repress it in a hierarchal manner.

At times a submitted prophecy is given almost immediately; another time it will be reserved until later in the service. On occasion the person submitting a "word" will be asked simply to receive it as for himself, not the body, or to reserve the word for another occasion as it doesn't seem to synchronize with this gathering.

The manifestation of the Holy Spirit gift of prophecy (1 Cor. 12:10) is given to profit the local assembly (1 Cor. 12:7; 14:3–4). It's the leader's task to administrate its exercise—to release the Spirit's grace, not control it—and see that order and edification are balanced. It will help any congregation to delight in and respond to prophecies—not grow to despise them.

Jack Hayford, "Despise Not Prophesying," *Ministries Today* (July/August 1989): 24.

The Leader's Edge

Every leader today needs more than just a theology regarding the dark realm of evil spirits and satanic bondage. It was the autumn of 1965 when I was first introduced to "deliverance ministry." Though biblically trained, and already with nine years in pastoral work, I still had nothing of experience in actual, personally confrontive ministry against them.[22] At that time of first instruction, I had no idea how much of an "edge" this understanding would bring to remaining decades of pastoral and leadership ministry. This article is only a door opener to the subject, but one worth venturing through in the light of God's Word and the Holy Spirit's wisdom in applying the victory of Calvary to human bondage.

For More...

The ministry of *Cleansing Stream* was born in the late 1980s at The Church On The Way. It is geared to be a resource in training pastors and church leaders for the ministry of deliverance.[23]

"The Finger of God" is a seventy-five-minute audiocassette with a companion fifty-page booklet prepared by Dr. Hayford outlining and detailing the foundational points of understanding regarding this demandingly needed ministry.

"Can a Christian Have a Freedom" is also available from Living Way Ministries.

[chapter 23] Setting People Free— the Way Jesus Does

"WHAT new doctrine is this!?!"

You can still hear the echo of the words nearly twenty centuries later. Even though Jesus didn't surrender to the criticism, the challenge seems to work. It seems that one of the adversary's most effective ways of neutralizing the will of many spiritual leaders to confront his dark kingdom with boldness is to suggest "Heresy!" The issue always boils down to one question—*not* "Do believers have authority over the demonic?", *but* "Do demons ever gain places of influence over believers?" The reality is, they do—and there is a sound-minded, biblical way to set believers free, and to do it the way Jesus does.

The Inaugural Case

In Mark's Gospel, Jesus' first occasion of teaching in the synagogue eventuates in His being confronted by a man in the congregation who challenges His ministry (Mark 1:21–28). Jesus confronts the demon motivating the man, and upon the man's being delivered, the question above is raised. The issue was not only one of amazement over Jesus' *authority,* but apparently also bewilderment over the fact that one of the local "church members" had been manipulated by a demonic presence. "They questioned," the Bible says, the traditional method of unbelief, which, finding itself powerless to function in the supernatural, employs the tactic of *doubt-filled inquiry* as a ruse to fault those who do. Opposition to this expression of Jesus' ministry followed Him, issuing in His extending teaching on the subject. (See Luke 11:14–26.) It also occasioned a warning when His starkest opponents neared the edge of ultimate blasphemy born of their criticism of His "deliverance" ministry. (See Matthew 12:22–32.)

Defining Terms

By "deliverance" I do not mean the broad and appropriate concept of "salvation" incorporated in *sodzo,* the Greek word for "to save, to heal, to deliver." Here I am referring to the specific concept of "freedom" contained in *aphesis,* the word used in Luke 4:18 where Jesus outlines the expressions inherent in Messiah's anointed ministry, including "deliverance to the captives." (This is from the King James Version. The New King James Version reads "liberty," and the New

International Version says "freedom to the prisoners.") In our Lord's own actions, as well as in these words, this specific arena of gospel ministry is designated and demonstrated. But the watershed point of definition is around the question, "Who may need 'deliverance'?" In short: "Sure," some say, "certain unsaved people may need demons cast out, but what about believers?"

Even though demonic oppression is manifestly abundant in its impact upon and influence through many believers, there are still a few supposedly "orthodox" resisters of this idea. The old seesaw argument goes, "How can the Holy Spirit and anything of the devil be in the same person?" James' instruction (James 3:6–18) and Paul's exhortations (2 Cor. 6:11–7:1; Gal. 5:1; Eph. 4:25–27; 2 Tim. 2:19–26) join to Peter's confrontation with Simon in Acts 8:13–23 to provide introductory evidence for the case: Demons *do* trouble and torment believers—and sometimes oppress them with burdensome bondage. *Clearly,* it would be improper to describe this oppression as "possession," but with equal certainty it would be foolish to deny the reality of the bondage. Worse still would be refusing or being unwilling to become equipped to minister to such soul-level affliction (usually mental or emotional, and often physical).

The Price of "Bothering"

I have long since learned the price of bothering to acknowledge the reality of the need for this area of ministry, much less offering any "deliverance" discipling resource in helping leaders to equip themselves and those they lead. While a host of *both* Pentecostal/Charismatic and evangelical/mainline leaders honestly deal with the scriptural verity of this problem and minister in various ways to bring freedom to precious believers, some tout their opposition as though such ministry was cultish or unbiblical. As with most arguments against Holy Spirit-empowered ministry, the paper tiger of a worst-cast scenario involving some freakish or idiosyncratic ministry is set up—and demolished—as evidence against the basic truth or value of "deliverance" ministry. Unfortunately, enough instances of undiscerning folly or arrogance-begetting-destructiveness exist to seem to justify closing the door on the subject.

However, a long trail of trusted, biblically sound, thoroughgoing teachers and ministers of the gospel have long since endorsed the need for ministering freedom to demon-tormented, oppressed or bound believers. When early discovering the vital need for and place of this aspect of Jesus' ministry being learned of and added to my own, how well I remember being assured and confirmed in my quest by a column in *Moody Monthly* magazine. It was there that the revered V. Raymond Edman, then president of Wheaton College, candidly discussed and affirmed the problem of demonic oppression/bondage in some believers, just as I am doing here. I don't know if he received similar "flak" or not, but if he did, I'm sure he knew he had chosen sides wisely *and scripturally* on this subject (Mark 9:38–40).

Committed to Discipling

I don't think I am generally perceived as a "deliverance" preacher or as a promoter of such. But the facts are:

- I have functioned in this arena of biblical ministry since 1965.
- Such ministry has always been a part of our congregation's life.
- A separate but associated national ministry of discipling leaders for "deliverance" ministry was born in our body-life and is still extended from this home base.

That I have avoided a reputation as someone anyone might think to be preoccupied with demons and the demonic is itself evidence for the relative place this feature of ministry has held.

It has neither been paramount or promoted *nor* denied or neglected. In line with Jesus' commission to teach and disciple, we have incorporated discipling for "deliverance" ministry in our patterns of training. (See Matthew 28:19–20; Mark 16:15–20.) Constantly at The Church On The Way, and now at The King's College and Seminary also, we see a component of essential discipleship is teaching potential leaders to function in "deliverance." In doing this, we prioritize a *manner* for such ministry—prioritizing discernment, wisdom and balance, joined to grace, love and tender good sense, rather than trumpeting high claims of "authority" or "power." The latter are both provided, of course, by the Holy Spirit's enablement of each believer's ministry. But we have chosen the course of focusing our sensitivities on the need of the *pained person* with whom we deal rather than on the *power given* for such ministry. To us, this seems consistent with Jesus' instructively balancing words yet non-prohibiting counsel to His disciples who had become initially distorted in their focus on the issue of "deliverance" ministry. (See Luke 10:17–24.)

An Advancing Awakening

As with many other features of Holy Spirit-filled-and-enabled ministry, the ministry of deliverance is finding wider and wiser acceptance and application.

The growing awareness of need for pastoral and leadership understanding and equipping in this arena has been acknowledged by virtually every quarter of Christ's body. Under the auspices of Mission America, a symposium on this theme was convened, resulting in affirming the essence of the issue as I present it here. Since this agency is an offspring of the respected Lausanne Committee of World Evangelism, it clearly indicates that the subject of demonic confrontation and the ministry of deliverance (including dealing with bondage in believers) is not an idea on a tangent, but a central feature of New Testament ministry. Added to this evidence is the fact that such widely diverse-on-the-evangelical-spectrum personalities as Neil Andersen, James Robison and Peter Wagner have each dealt with the subject candidly—and realistically.

I want to encourage leaders who have been fearful or intimidated by the subject to move out of the shadows of uncertainty. There are increasing and reliable resources that can provide discerning understanding and a pastoral atmosphere for the ministry of deliverance. Taken together, these facts are calling you and me, as pastors, to recognize the Spirit's call to awareness and action at this time. Why? Because according to the Word, "The devil has come down to you, having great wrath, because he knows that he has a short time" (Rev. 12:12). This being the case, we need to be ready to confront him at every point and with all the resources *and the honesty* that is ready to acknowledge two things:

1. **The battle and the bondage impact believers as well as unbelievers.**
2. **The Spirit and the Word are adequate to enable our effectively answering the challenge.**

When the reality of human bondage meets Christ's answer of delivering grace, the results will always be victorious for those serve and glorifying to Him whom we serve.

Jack Hayford, "Demons, Deliverance, Discernment," *Ministries Today* (July/August 1999): 22–23.

[conclusion] A Leader's Prayer: "That Your Life May Flow Through Me"

Let me walk today, O Jesus, in a purity of love,
That I might reveal Your character in everything I do;
Seeing every situation from the view of heaven above,
So Your life may flow through me.

Let me speak today, O Jesus, with a measure to my words
That will show by tone and content that my tongue is Christ the
    Lord's;
Idle words all disappearing—vital wisdom-words replace—
So Your Word may flow through me.

Let me touch today, O Jesus, with a gentleness and health,
That with every contact afterward, the wholeness and the wealth
Left deposited, reveal Jehovah-Rapha passed that way;
Let Your power flow through me.

Let me think today, O Jesus—with a clarity of mind,
That is rinsed of human reasoning—all fogginess behind;
Heaven's sunlight so pervading all my viewpoints—all my thoughts;
That Your mind abide in me.

Here I bow today, O Jesus—I present my sacrifice,
As I worship You, my Savior, offering all I have of life.
Pour Your Spirit on this altar—now consume with holy fire,
So Your light may shine through me.

Now I rise today, O Jesus—let these blessings all combine;
May all heavenly graces manifest, fulfilling Your design,
For this child cries, "Abba, Father," work Your will—in Jesus' name,
Til Your kingdom come through me.

—JACK W. HAYFORD
JULY 28, 1999

Poem first published in this book

[notes]

1. *Billy Graham—God's Ambassador,* a pictorial published by Time-Life books (Minneapolis, MN: Billy Graham Evangelistic Association, 1999); Billy Graham, *Just As I Am* (New York: HarperCollins, 1997).

2. John Pollock, *Billy Graham—the Authorized Biography* (New York: McGraw-Hill, 1966); William Martin, *A Prophet With Honor: The Billy Graham Story* (New York: William Morrow and Co., 1992).

3. Howard Snyder, *Radical Renewal: The Problem of Wineskins Today* (n.p.: Touch Outreach Ministries, 1996).

4. Jack W. Hayford, *Anhelo De Plenitud (A Passion for Fullness)* (Nashville, TN: Editorial Caribe, 1999).

5. Eugene Peterson, *A Long Obedience in the Same Direction* (Westmont, IL: Intervarsity Press, 2000).

6. Author's note: The material in chapters ten and eleven were left "as is," dated to the time they were written in the early 1990s. Unless seen in their historical context, I feel they would lack the critical "edge" I hope to convey—even now.

7. "Wand'ring Tho'ts" by Jack W. Hayford. Copyright © 1985.

8. Jack W. Hayford, *Our Daily Walk* (n.p.: Sovereign World Ltd., 2000).

9. For more information, visit Gary Smalley's website at smalleyonline.com for more information. You can also write his offices at 1482 Lake Shore Drive, Branson, MO 65616. The phone number is (800) 84-TODAY.

10. For more information on SonScape Re-Creation Ministries,

phone (719) 687-7007 or (888) SON-SCAPE. You can also write them at P. O. Box 7777, Woodland Park, CO 80866-7777; their e-mail address is sonscape@usa.net.

11. For more information on *Consultation IV,* call (818) 779-8040.

12. You can subscribe from their website at christianhistory.net or by contacting their offices at *Christian History,* 465 Gundersen Dr., Carol Stream, IL 60188.

13. Joy Dawson, *Forever Ruined for the Ordinary* (Nashville: Thomas Nelson, 2000).

14. "In the Garden" by C. Austin Miles. Public domain.

15. Lamar Boschman Ministries, The Worship Institute, P. O. Box 130, Bedford, TX 76095; phone, (817) 281-5255; website, www.lamarboschman.com.

16. Jack W. Hayford, *Worship His Majesty* (Ventura, CA: Regal Books, 1987, 2000).

17. Editor's note: The reader may already be aware that Pastor Hayford has composed over six hundred worship songs and hymns—many in wide circulation, the most renowned being "Majesty," which today is one of Christianity's most widely sung songs globally. Abundant biblical teaching resources on worship are also available.

18. Jack Hayford, *The Key to Everything* (Lake Mary, FL: Charisma House, 1993).

19. These articles by Dr. Nathaniel Van Cleave are found threaded through key texts in *The Spirit-Filled Life Bible* (Jack W. Hayford, general editor; Nashville: Thomas Nelson Publishers, 1999). They are also included in the encyclopedic section of *Hayford's Bible Handbook* (Nashville, TN: Thomas Nelson Publishers, 1995).

20. Editor's note: Free use of this statement is granted provided that appropriate copyright is indicated: "I Believe in God's Will to Heal," copyright © 1988, Jack W. Hayford, Van Nuys, California, USA.

21. Wayne Grudem, *The Gift of Prophecy in the New Testament and Today* (Wheaton, IL: Crossway Books, 2001).

22. My introduction and instruction were provided through two faithful missionary couples—John and Jean Firth, with Arthur and Evelyn Thompson. These had, respectively, been used mightily by the Holy Spirit in Colombia and the Philippine Islands, establishing hundreds of churches and extending the kingdom of God into hitherto unpenetrated areas.

23. This ministry is a trustworthy point of resourcing and training in this special area of evangelism and pastoral work. You can contact them at P. O. Box 7076, Van Nuys, CA 91409-7076; (818) 678-6888 or (800) 580-8190. Their website is cleansingstream.org.

Get **Grounded** *in the Word*
with Pastor Jack

Explore some of the biblical resources produced under Dr. Hayford's writing and editorial leadership:

Dr. Jack Hayford, Founder,
The King's College & Seminary

The Spirit-Filled Life Bible
An insight-filled study Bible presenting prophetic and practical help for Christian life and service

Spirit-Filled Life Study Guides
38 separate 160-page interactive studies focusing on individual books of the Bible, plus topical studies providing practical application of important spiritual principles

Hayford's Bible Handbook
A study resource that uniquely unveils "Kingdom Keys" to Scripture; a wealth of valuable information and a spiritual stimulus that will encourage faith, growth and Spirit-filled service to Christ as you explore His Word

For more information on these or other helpful resources by Jack Hayford, visit www.jackhayford.com. There you may:

- Purchase from over 40 books and 1500 tapes by Jack Hayford, including:
  - *Worship His Majesty, The Beauty of Spiritual Language*
  - *A Passion for Fullness, Living the Spirit-Formed Life*
- Listen to the Living Way Ministries radio and television program
- Receive information about Dr. Hayford's upcoming events
  — *and* —
- Investigate The King's College and Seminary, founded by Dr. Jack Hayford
  - Call **1-888-779-8040** for more information about this rapidly growing center equipping Word-centered, Spirit-filled leaders.
  - Undergraduate and graduate programs (recognized by the U.S. Department of Education, TRACS and AABC) are available through online, on-campus and modular intensive formats.
  - **The Jack W. Hayford School of Pastoral Nurture** is a 6-day interactive intensive with Pastor Hayford for the continued education and enrichment of senior pastors from all backgrounds.

14800 Sherman Way, Van Nuys, CA 91405 • 888-779-8040 • www.jackhayford.com

If you enjoyed *The Leading Edge,* here are some others titles from Charisma House that we think will minister to you...

Taking Our Cities for God
John Dawson
ISBN: 0-88419-764-8
Retail Price: $13.99

This book invites you to take part in a spiritual clean-up program that will change you and your community forever! *Taking Our Cities for God* offers a revised and detailed action plan that will open the heavens and allow God's blessings to flow freely.

The Missions Addiction
David Shibley
ISBN: 0-88419-772-7
Retail Price: $13.99

In these action-packed pages, you will discover a Global Jesus Generation that is creating discomfort in the church and change in missions worldwide. God is calling you to become part of a contagious epidemic of missions-hearted believers who will bring global fame to His name!

The Burden of Freedom
Myles Munroe
ISBN: 0-88419-783-2
Retail Price: $19.99

Dr. Myles Munroe brings a new understanding to the word *freedom.* The importance of building good management skills is defined through examples of stewardship. With any new freedom come additional responsibility and challenges that impact and change the course of history.

Charisma HOUSE
Books about Spirit-Led Living

To pick up a copy of any of these titles, contact your local Christian bookstore or order online at www.charismawarehouse.com.